The Luke Experiment

How Luke's Gospel
can help you know Jesus better

by
Andrew Page

VTR
Publications

ISBN 978-3-95776-146-0

Author photo on the back cover:
(c) Roger Eldridge Photography, www.eldridgephotos.com

Cover design: Chris Allcock / VTR Publications

Contents

Acknowledgements

I am very grateful to Thomas Mayer at VTR for agreeing to publish this book. And Chris Allcock has, once again, done a great job with the section drawings and the cover design.

A number of people read the manuscript and gave me their comments and suggestions, so I am glad to thank them here: Paul Allcock, Graham Ball, Jenny Goon, Gerhild Haitchi, Jo Harkrader, Biddy Taylor, Charlie Watkins and Wolfgang Widmann.

I have many friends who have prayed for me in the writing of this book: I owe them a huge debt. Many of them (but not all) are part of Above Bar Church, Southampton: I would be a lesser person without my church family.

This is a book I thought I could never write. After writing about the Gospels of Mark, John and Matthew, I wanted to write about Luke, too, but I couldn't find a learnable structure. But that has changed. Now I am loving meditating my way through Luke's Gospel and so getting to know Jesus better.

I am praying that many other people will experience the same thing.

To God be the glory!

Andrew Page
andrew@themarkdrama.com

My Introduction: Invitation to an Experiment

This is a book about two things at once.

First, it's about learning the Gospel of Luke. Luke addressed his Gospel to someone called Theophilus (see chapter 1:3), but I'm sure he wanted his book to reach a much wider audience. And most of those people would not have read the Gospel but listened to it: few people in the first century could have expected to own a copy for themselves. So Luke wrote it so people could memorize it. Not word for word, but bit by bit – so they could get to know Jesus better and tell the story to others.

So, second, this is a book about rediscovering Jesus. You may already know Luke's Gospel very well, or you may just be starting out: but as we spend time together in his book the aim will be that we will get to admire, love and enjoy Jesus more. If that's what you want, you've come to the right place.

So that's what the experiment is about: learning the Gospel so we can get to know Jesus better. I hope you will try it out for yourself.

Please take time to read the rest of this introduction. It won't take you long, but it will help you get the maximum out of *The Luke Experiment.*

The Title Page of Luke's Gospel (Luke 1:1-4)

The first paragraph in the Gospel is Luke giving us a heads-up as to what's coming. What we're going to read is not new, because *many have undertaken to draw up an account of the things that have been fulfilled among us* (1).

But Luke's Gospel is the result of painstaking research: he has *carefully investigated everything from the beginning* (3a). Luke is not claiming to have been there and seen all of this for himself; rather he has talked to *those who from the first were eyewitnesses and servants of the word* (2).

The result of the research is that Luke *decided to write an orderly account* (3b). This doesn't mean that the Gospel is in chronological order: that's especially clear in Luke's central section (chapter 9:51 – 19:27).

Luke may mean that he has written in thematic order, grouping incidents together that cover the same topic.

But he may well be signalling, too, that he has written his Gospel with a literary structure, which will enable his audience to commit the Jesus story to memory. (For a little more on this, see Appendix One, Questions 1, 2 and 3.)

And Luke tells Theophilus *why* he has written his Gospel: it's *so that you may know the certainty of the things you have been taught* (4). What Theophilus has been told about Jesus is not a made-up story: this is history, and there is evidence to support it.

The good news about Jesus is true.

Luke wants all of us who read his Gospel to be sure of that too.

The Structure of Luke's Gospel

It looks like Luke has structured his Gospel with blocks of five incidents each.

There are twenty-five such blocks in all, in eight different sections.

Look, for example, at Section One, which runs from chapter 3:1 to chapter 6:11. Here is the structure as I see it:

A. The foundation of Jesus' ministry (3:1 – 4:30)
   1. John: his identity and message (3:1-20)
   2. Jesus: his baptism (3:21-22)
   3. Jesus: his genealogy (3:23-38)
   4. Jesus: his temptation (4:1-13)
   5. Jesus: his identity and message (4:14-30)

B. The beginning of Jesus' ministry (4:31 – 5:16)
   1. Jesus drives out an evil spirit (4:31-37)
   2. Jesus heals Simon's mother-in-law and others (4:38-41)
   3. Jesus says his priority is preaching (4:42-44)
   4. Jesus calls the first disciples (5:1-11)
   5. Jesus heals a leper (5:12-16)

C. The opposition to Jesus' ministry (5:17 – 6:11)
   1. Jesus forgives and heals a paralysed man (5:17-26)
   2. Jesus calls Levi and eats with sinners (5:27-32)
   3. Jesus predicts a radical break with Judaism (5:33-39)
   4. Jesus is Lord of the Sabbath (6:1-5)
   5. Jesus provokes opposition by healing on the Sabbath (6:6-11)

There are four things to notice about this structure:

1. The whole section has a main theme

The theme of Section One is *Introducing Jesus*. We meet Jesus as an adult for the first time, and the section as a whole gives us an initial insight into who Jesus is, what he does, and the opposition he encounters.

And each section, throughout the Gospel, has its own theme which focuses on Jesus.

2. The section contains blocks of five incidents each

Section One has three of these blocks. The number of blocks varies from section to section, but all of them point to Jesus. And it's always true that every block contains five incidents.

3. I have given each block-of-five a heading

You can see my headings for Section One's three blocks above. Each heading is my suggestion of what binds together the five incidents. If you don't agree with me, I have no problem with that: feel free to find a heading which fits better in your opinion.

And I have provided a heading for all twenty-five blocks-of-five throughout the whole Gospel.

(For the complete outline of my structure of Luke's Gospel, see Appendix 3.)

4. The section can easily be learnt by heart

This is not about learning every word, but simply the order of the events in the section.

This is true despite the fact that the sections vary in length. But even the longer sections (which have four blocks-of-five) can be easily committed to memory.

Most people can learn the order of the incidents in a section in under fifteen minutes.

But why should I learn Luke's Gospel by heart?

That's a great question. But there are some very good reasons:

I. Because the Bible is the word of God it has remarkable power. We often forget this. In Psalm 119:11 David says to God: *I have hidden your word in my heart that I might not sin against you.*

II. Because Luke has written his Gospel to make this easy. Even though the length of each section varies, you will notice how easy it is to learn each individual block-of-five. My guess is that the Holy Spirit led Luke to write this way because he wants us to have his word in our hearts.

III.   Because learning the Gospel in this way makes it possible to do Bible study in the shower without getting your Bible wet! Of course I normally have my Bible with me when I am doing Bible study, but sometimes it's brilliant to meditate on the Bible just using your memory. So as you are walking down the road you can tell yourself the Gospel events and begin talking to Jesus about what you are remembering.

IV.   Because I would love you to experience what I have experienced. I confess that I have always struggled rather with Luke's Gospel: I have loved the famous bits of course, such as the parable of the lost son, and the encounter with the risen Jesus on the road to Emmaus. However, I have never been able to get my head round *the whole thing*. But now, with this structure in my mind, I am able to meditate my way through the book. The Holy Spirit is using Luke's Gospel to help my love for Jesus to grow. And that makes me want to share this with others.

How to use this book

This book is like a basic commentary, but one you can read through rather than just using for reference. As we look at each of the eight sections of Luke there'll be an introduction called *Enjoying the View*: this provides the structure and the main theme of the section.

Next comes *Unpacking the Content.* Here I look at each block in the section in turn, explaining the incidents and so teaching through that part of Luke's Gospel.

Then I make some suggestions as to how you could memorize the section (this is called *Learning the Gospel*). Most people aren't used to learning by heart, but it really is worth it. And remember we're not talking about learning every word but the order of events in the section. The headings I've suggested for each block-of-five make this easier to do. There are some simple learning tips in the box on page 25.

One good way of getting the learning done is to team up with a friend. You agree to both read through, say, Section One and learn the order of events. Then you meet up to go for a walk or have a coffee, and re-tell the section together (see My Conclusion, point 3, page 177, for more details). Doing this with a friend will help you to do the learning rather than just skip it!

The last part is called *Meeting the Lord.* This is a reminder of the reason we are doing all this: we want to rediscover Jesus. As you talk to the Lord about what you remember from what you have been reading, you will start knowing, admiring and loving him more.

Please don't read *The Luke Experiment* too quickly. You might want to take a week over each of the eight sections, so that you have time to let what you are reading sink in. If you and a friend are both trying the experiment, you might meet up once a week to tell one another the stories and to talk about Jesus.

Thank you for reading my introduction; now it's time to read Luke's.

I am praying that everyone who reads this book will enjoy Luke's Gospel and enjoy meeting Jesus. The Luke experiment starts now...

Luke's Introduction
Luke 1:1 – 2:52

It seems natural to conclude that Luke's introduction to his Gospel covers the first two chapters: there is a gap of about 18 years between the end of chapter 2 and the start of chapter 3.

Unlike Mark, Luke decides to go back to Jesus' birth and childhood. In his introduction he shows us two things: God has gone to great lengths to prepare for Jesus' coming into the world, and he is already revealing the identity of the child.

Jesus is the Messiah, the Saviour God promised through the Old Testament prophets. And he's the Son of God.

He deserves our worship.

Enjoying the View

Luke's title page (1:1-4)

A. Before the birth of Jesus (1:5-80)

1. The birth of John the Baptist announced (1:5-25)
2. The birth of Jesus announced (1:26-38)
3. Mary visits Elizabeth (1:39-56)
4. The birth of John the Baptist (1:57-66)
5. Zechariah prophesies and praises God (1:67-80)

B. The birth and boyhood of Jesus (2:1-52)

1. The birth of Jesus (2:1-7)
2. What the angel says (2:8-21)
3. What Simeon says (2:22-35)
4. What Anna says (2:36-40)
5. The boyhood of Jesus (2:41-52)

It would be good to take time to read through Luke's Introduction. For many of us most of what we read will be very familiar: let's be praying that God will open our eyes to see Jesus more clearly. And that we'll *feel* something.

Wonder.

Because that's part of what the experiment is about.

Unpacking the Content

Luke's title page (1:1-4)

For my comments on Luke's opening paragraph, see *My Introduction*, page 7.

A. Before the birth of Jesus (1:5-80)

Luke starts as he means to go on: before telling us about the birth of Jesus he gives us five incidents which lead up to it. And the message is clear: God is at work.

1. – The birth of John the Baptist announced (1:5-25)

God wants to reveal to Zechariah (and to us) that he is providing someone who will *make ready a people prepared for the Lord* (17b).

There are four stages in what God is doing here.

First, he prepares the way (5-10). Zechariah and Elizabeth have no children and are *very old* (7b). But despite the disappointment they've experienced, both of them are *righteous in the sight of God, observing all the Lord's commands and decrees blamelessly* (6).

Zechariah is a priest, and is chosen by lot *to go into the temple of the Lord and burn incense* (9). This involves going into the sanctuary (which is not the same as the holy of holies). So Zechariah has gone inside, while *all the assembled worshippers were praying outside* (10b).

God has set everything up so that Zechariah can experience the most important thing that has ever happened to him.

Second, he reveals the plan (11-17). The angel Gabriel appears and tells Zechariah: *Your wife Elizabeth will bear you a son, and you are to call him John* (13). And this won't be just any boy: *he will be great in the sight of the Lord* (15).

Now Gabriel tells Zechariah that John *will be filled with the Holy Spirit even before he is born* (15). It's hard to imagine what's going through Zechariah's mind: surely he must realise that there is more to come.

And there is: *He will bring back many of the people of Israel to the Lord their God* (16) and *make ready a people prepared for the Lord* (17b). And he will do this *in the spirit and power of Elijah* (17a).

Zechariah will already be thinking of the prophecy of Malachi (see Mal 4:5-6) and realising that Gabriel is saying that the son he and Elizabeth will have will bring about a religious revival in Israel.

Perhaps this sounds like it's too good to be true.

So God does something else.

Third, he punishes the unbelief (18-22). Zechariah just can't believe it. He and his wife are too old to have a child anyway, so he is sceptical: *How can I be sure of this?* (18). He is probably asking for a sign.

So Gabriel tells Zechariah that he will be *not able to speak until the day this happens, because you did not believe my words* (20). God is punishing Zechariah's unbelief.

But he is doing something else too. After Zechariah has come out of the sanctuary, the worshippers outside realise he's had a divine encounter of some kind *for he kept making signs to them but remained unable to speak* (22b).

This is not only punishment. It's also a sign to Zechariah that this whole thing is true. He had asked for a sign (see 18); now he's getting it.

So it's obvious what God is going to do at the end of the story.

Fourth, he keeps the promise (23-25). Luke tells us that *Elizabeth became pregnant* (24) and says *The Lord has done this for me* (25).

Zechariah and Elizabeth will never be the same again.

So the birth of the baby who will become John the Baptist has been announced. But before we read about the birth itself, Luke tells us about another announcement.

2. – The birth of Jesus announced (1:26-38)

This is Gabriel again, sent by God to give Mary news that will not only change *her* life: it will change the world.

Luke shows us at each stage how Mary reacts.

First, she's frightened (26-29). Gabriel goes to Nazareth and appears to her. He says *Greetings, you who are highly favoured! The Lord is with you* (28).

What does Luke tell us about Mary? She's *pledged to be married* to Joseph (27): this would last a year, during which time the couple would not sleep together. So Luke wants us to know that Mary is a virgin (27, twice).

There is one detail we're told about Joseph: he's *a descendant of David* (27).

Mary doesn't yet know *why* the angel has appeared to her, but, understandably, she is *greatly troubled at his words* (29). That probably means she's just plain frightened.

But this is just the start for Mary.

Second, she's puzzled (30-34). The reason is that Gabriel tells her that she *will conceive and give birth to a son* (31).

So Mary asks *How will this be, […] since I am a virgin?* (34).

We don't know how much she grasps of what the angel tells her about the child she's going to have. He *will be called the Son of the Most High* (32), God will *give him the throne of his father David* (32), and *his kingdom will never end* (33).

Does Mary realise that these promises are a fulfilment of God's words to King David through the prophet Nathan? David was promised a descendant of whom God could say *I will be his father, and he shall be my son* (2 Sam 7:14); and God added that *your kingdom shall endure for ever* (2 Sam 7:16).

If Mary is registering all this, it will only have deepened her puzzlement.

So Gabriel explains.

Third, she's humble (35-38). Mary clearly decides to trust this angelic announcement. She has an announcement of her own: she is *the Lord's servant* (38).

This humble response comes after hearing how it's going to be possible for her to have a child when she's not sleeping with Joseph. Gabriel speaks these astonishing words: *The Holy Spirit will come on you, and the power of the Most High will overshadow you* (35a).

Mary is going to conceive while still a virgin.

The problem for most of us is that we've read this before. But it should stop us in our tracks.

And now Mary learns *why* God is going to do this: it's *so the holy one to be born will be called the Son of God* (35b).

She has already been told what name the child is to have: she is *to call him Jesus* (31). Now she hears that baby Jesus will be the son of Mary and the Son of God.

Human *and* divine.

It looks like Mary has begun to believe this, and she's going to get confirmation that it's all true, because *even Elizabeth your relative is going to have a child in her old age* (36).

Gabriel has delivered the message he was sent with. He ends by reassuring Mary that *no word from God will ever fail* (37).

And Mary, humbly, replies *May your word to me be fulfilled* (38).

Luke has shown us the journey Mary has been on during her encounter with the angel Gabriel: first she's frightened, then she's puzzled, and finally she's humble.

What Mary does next is exactly what we would expect.

3. – Mary visits Elizabeth (1:39-56)

It's probably a seventy-mile journey from Nazareth to the home of Zechariah and Elizabeth, and Mary is determined to get there.

When she does, two things happen.

First, confirmation (39-45). God is going to convince both of these women that he is at work here.

The reaction of her baby to Mary's arrival confirms something for Elizabeth, for *when Elizabeth heard Mary's greeting, the baby leaped in her womb* (41).

Elizabeth's pregnancy confirms something for Mary, too: if what Gabriel had said about her elderly relative being pregnant is true, that means that what he'd said about Mary is also true.

But there's more confirmation for Mary. Elizabeth, now *filled with the Holy Spirit* (41), calls out *Blessed are you among women, and blessed is the child you will bear!* (42).

She tells Mary about her baby leaping for joy and asks *Why am I so favoured, that the mother of my Lord should come to me?* (43).

Those are extraordinary words: Mary is *the mother of my Lord* (43).

No wonder Elizabeth calls out *Blessed is she who has believed that the Lord would fulfil his promises to her!* (45).

So now Mary and Elizabeth are more certain than ever that God is doing something wonderful here: he is confirming the truth of it all.

And that leads to something else.

Second, celebration (46-56). Mary's heart is overflowing with praise to God: *My soul glorifies the Lord and my spirit rejoices in God my Saviour* (46-47).

Maybe the Holy Spirit is reminding Mary of Hannah's prayer (see 1 Sam 2:1-10); he is certainly filling her with joy.

There is joy at what God has done: *The Mighty One has done great things for me* (49).

There is joy at what God always does: *His mercy extends to those who fear him* (50). And he overturns human expectations: *He has brought down rulers from their thrones but has lifted up the humble* (52).

There's more: *He has filled the hungry with good things but has sent the rich away empty* (53).

And there's another reason why Mary is celebrating. God is fulfilling his plan: *He has helped his servant Israel, remembering to be merciful to Abraham and his descendants for ever, just as he promised our ancestors* (54-55).

When we become convinced of God's good plan for us and for the world, the natural response is celebration and worship.

Mary's visit to Elizabeth will be unforgettable. She stays there *for about three months and then returned home* (56).

4. – The birth of John the Baptist (1:57-66)

This is a wonderful story, which ends with Zechariah exploding with joy and praising God.

First, the birth (57-58). Luke wants us to know that what has happened to Elizabeth meets with general approval: *her neighbours and relatives heard that the Lord had shown her great mercy, and they shared her joy* (58).

Second, the naming (59-63). Everyone expects the baby to be named after his father. But somehow Zechariah has communicated to Elizabeth what the angel in the temple had told him about the naming of their child (see chapter 1:13).

So she tells everyone that *he is to be called John* (60). Because of the surprise of family and friends, Zechariah has to be asked for his opinion. There it is, on the writing tablet, plain for all to see: *His name is John* (63).

Third, the reaction (64-66). Suddenly Zechariah doesn't need a writing tablet any longer: *he began to speak, praising God* (64).

Everyone is *filled with awe* (65) and is asking *What then is this child going to be?* (66).

They don't know the answer, but Zechariah, Elizabeth and we do: he is going to *make ready a people prepared for the Lord* (chapter 1:17b).

5. – Zechariah prophesies and praises God (1:67-80)

Because he is now filled with the Holy Spirit, Zechariah bursts out into praise. He has two topics in mind.

First, the coming of the Messiah (68-75). As far as we know, Gabriel had not mentioned the Messiah when Zechariah encountered him in the temple. But the old priest is so certain of the Messiah's arrival that he talks about it as if it had already happened: God *has come to his people* (68) and *has raised up a horn of salvation for us* (69).

This is all because God remembers his covenant with Israel: he had made promises *to our father Abraham* (73); the Messiah who brings salvation is from *the house of his servant David* (69). What is happening now is the fulfilment of God's plan for his people.

And the Messiah will make possible a new relationship with God: he will *enable us to serve him without fear in holiness and righteousness before him all our days* (74b-75).

But, understandably, there is something else Zechariah's thinking about.

Second, the work of the forerunner (76-79). Zechariah is sure that John is going to be a prophet who will *go on before the Lord to prepare the way for him* (76).

John's aim will be *to give his people the knowledge of salvation through the forgiveness of their sins* (77): this is how he will prepare the way for God.

But now Zechariah is focusing on the Messiah again: he describes the Coming One in ways which remind us that God is fulfilling his promises. *The rising sun will come to us from heaven* (78, see Mal 4:2) and the Messiah will *shine on those living in darkness and in the shadow of death* (79, see Isa 9:2).

After Zechariah's praise poem is over, Luke gives us a preview of John's future by telling us that *the child grew and became strong in spirit; and he lived in the wilderness until he appeared publicly to Israel* (80).

At the end of this first block of five incidents it's difficult to stop reading. Everything has been pointing forwards to the birth of the promised Messiah.

Luke has given us two angelic announcements of unexpected births, and, as a result, two expressions of praise. But he has only told us about the historical event of *one* of the births: Zechariah and Elizabeth's son John.

So we move to the second block-of-five.

B. The birth and boyhood of Jesus (2:1-52)

1. – The birth of Jesus (2:1-7)

This short paragraph tells us about the birth of the Son of God. There are two things worth focusing on.

First, the background (1-5). Luke's mention of the Roman census is not easy to fit in with known history (1-2, see the longer commentaries for details).

But, because *everyone went to their own town to register* (3), Joseph goes to Bethlehem, taking Mary with him. He is just obeying the law, but the general expectation was that the Messiah would be born there (see John 7:42 and Mic 5:2).

In the Greek original there is no mention of an inn. Because Bethlehem is Joseph's ancestral home, it is very likely that the couple are staying with relatives.

Luke reminds us of two things. Mary *was pledged to be married to him and was expecting a child* (5). So we're to remember that Mary is a virgin; and that she's pregnant.

And heaven holds its breath.

Second, the event (6-7). Luke tells us that Mary *gave birth to her firstborn, a son* (7a).

It's happened. The eternal Son of God has taken on humanity: he is also the son of Mary.

That Mary *wrapped him in cloths and placed him in a manger* (7) doesn't mean that this all takes place in a stable; in an ordinary village home there would be mangers at the side of the family's living room.

This extraordinary event is simply told, but it should fill us with astonished gratitude.

2. – What the angel says (2:8-21)

The shepherds looking after their flocks get the shock of their lives: *an angel of the Lord appeared to them* (9).

Luke identifies for us the main players in a field outside Bethlehem.

First, the angel (8-12). The message the angel brings is *good news that will cause great joy for all the people* (10). The focus is on the nation of Israel.

But the most important part of this good news is that it's about salvation: *Today in the town of David a Saviour has been born to you* (11a). And the angel tells the shepherds exactly who this Saviour is: *he is the Messiah, the Lord* (11b).

The Messiah is the rescuer promised in the Old Testament scriptures. And the baby is not *a* Lord, but *the* Lord: this is God himself coming to visit his people.

And the angel gives the shepherds *a sign* (12a): they *will find a baby wrapped in cloths and lying in a manger* (12b). A baby wrapped in cloths is hardly unusual; but when they see the baby is in a manger, the shepherds will know that the message about the Saviour is true.

Second, the angels (13-14). Now, instead of just one angel, there's *a great company of the heavenly host* (13). They praise God and say *Glory to God in the highest heaven, and on earth peace to those on whom his favour rests* (14).

With such astonishing news, silence is out of the question.

Third, the shepherds (15-20). They rush into Bethlehem and find *Mary and Joseph, and the baby, who was lying in the manger* (16).

The sign has been fulfilled: the fact that the baby is in a manger means that the angel's message can be relied upon. So, inevitably, *they spread the word concerning what had been told them about this child* (17).

Everyone is amazed (see 18) and Mary *treasured up all these things and pondered them in her heart* (19).

And it looks like the shepherds have been changed for ever: they are *praising God for all the things they had heard and seen, which were just as they had been told* (20). Once again we see the importance of that sign: it had put everything beyond doubt (see 12, 16, 20).

Luke tells us that *when it was time to circumcise the child, he was named Jesus* (21a). And he reminds us that Jesus is *the name the angel had given him before he was conceived* (21b, and see chapter 1:31).

Joseph and Mary are determined to carry out Gabriel's instructions.

There is so much in chapter 2:8-21. But the most important part of it is the explanation from *an angel of the Lord* (9) as to the identity of Jesus: he's the Saviour, the Messiah and the Lord (see 11).

3. – What Simeon says (2:22-35)

Joseph and Mary take Jesus to the temple in Jerusalem, because he is forty days old: it's time for *the purification rites required by the Law of Moses* (22).

But it's clear that the most important thing that happens to them in the temple is their encounter with Simeon and Anna.

Simeon, *righteous and devout* (25a), is *waiting for the consolation of Israel* (25b): he's looking forward to the arrival of the Messiah. And imagine this: *it had been revealed to him by the Holy Spirit that he would not die before he had seen the Lord's Messiah* (26).

That is an extraordinary sentence. Every morning Simeon must have got up with the question in his mind *Is it going to be today?*

Luke mentions the Holy Spirit three times in three verses (see 25-27), and the Spirit must have given Simeon a nudge when he saw Jesus: he *took him in his arms and praised God* (28).

What Simeon says should fill us with wonder.

He tells God that he is now ready to die (see 29): in other words, he is sure that this baby is the Messiah. He spells it out: *My eyes have seen your salvation* (30). Jesus is the Saviour.

And not just for Israel: this baby is *a light for revelation to the Gentiles* (32), so this is for *all nations* (31).

In Isaiah's prophecy in the Old Testament, God had said this to his Servant: *It is too small a thing for you to be my servant to restore the tribes of Jacob (...). I will also make you a light for the Gentiles, that my salvation may reach to the ends of the earth* (Isa 49:6, see also Isa 42:6).

So this baby is not only the Messiah; he is also the Servant of the Lord. However much or little Joseph and Mary have understood, they *marvelled at what was said about him* (33).

So should we.

But Simeon isn't finished yet. After blessing the couple, he warns Mary that Jesus will meet with opposition: he will be *a sign that will be spoken against* (34), so that *the thoughts of many hearts will be revealed* (35a).

One day Jesus will say the same thing himself (see chapter 12:49-53).

And there is something else that Mary needs to hear. Simeon tells her that *a sword will pierce your own soul too* (35b). There are no details but the message is clear: what happens to Jesus will cause great suffering to Mary.

If we take Simeon's words seriously, we are understanding more and more about who Jesus is and what he will do.

But there is more to come.

4. – What Anna says (2:36-40)

Luke tells us more about Anna than he had about Simeon. Apart from being *very old* (36) and a widow (see 36b-37a), she is from *the tribe of Asher* (36).

The northern kingdom of Israel had long ceased to exist, and Asher was one of the most northerly tribes in that kingdom. But it looks like Luke wants us to see that Jesus is not only welcomed by Simeon from the south-ern kingdom of Judah, but also by a representative from the north.

Anna sees Jesus and thanks God: she *spoke about the child to all who were looking forward to the redemption of Jerusalem* (38).

While Simeon's main focus was on *all nations* (31), while not forgetting *your people Israel* (32), Anna is thinking of blessing for Israel.

Joseph and Mary return north to Nazareth (see 39). And Luke sums up the next twelve years by telling us that *the child grew and became strong; he was filled with wisdom, and the grace of God was on him* (40).

We would love to know more about those twelve years. But in Bethlehem and in Jerusalem we have learnt important things: who Jesus is and why he has come into the world.

And Luke has prepared the way for what is to come.

5. – The boyhood of Jesus (2:41-52)

Joseph and Mary, with Jesus, have been in Jerusalem for the Passover Fes-tival. Now they are on their way home (see 41-43).

But Jesus isn't with them.

The women think he's with the men. The men think he's with the women. That's the trouble when you're *twelve years old* (42).

So when they realise he's gone missing, they go back to Jerusalem to look for him. Luke gives us the news: *After three days they found him in the temple courts, sitting among the teachers, listening to them and asking them questions* (46).

And everyone is *amazed at his understanding and his answers* (47). So Jesus isn't just asking questions; he's giving answers too.

But his most important answer is not to the religious teachers, but to his mother. When she asks him *Son, why have you treated us like this?* (48), Jesus replies *Why were you searching for me? […] Didn't you know I had to be in my Father's house?* (49).

Jesus is puzzled that his parents haven't realised that God is his Father. Already, as a twelve-year-old, he is aware that he has a unique relationship with God.

Luke tells us that Joseph and Mary *did not understand what he was saying to them* (50): have they forgotten what they were told by angels around the time of Jesus' birth?

But Mary *treasured all these things in her heart* (51b).

Jesus is *obedient* to his parents (51a). And, says Luke, he *grew in wisdom and stature, and in favour with God and man* (52).

We have reached the end of Luke's Introduction. He has told us about the lead-up to Jesus' birth, the birth itself, and what others say about his identity.

And, in the only story we are told about Jesus' childhood, he tells us himself who he is: the Son of God.

As we consider the first recorded words of Jesus in any of the Gospels (see 49), it will prompt us to worship him.

Learning the Gospel

First, learn *Luke's title page* and the two other headings in bold: they will help you to remember what is coming in each block. Then go back and learn each block's five incidents. As you do, many of the details will come back to you.

You will find this easier to do if you have arranged with a friend to meet up after you have both learnt *Luke's Introduction.*

This is not difficult, but it is so worthwhile.

Luke's Introduction

Luke's title page

A. Before the birth of Jesus
1. The birth of John the Baptist announced
2. The birth of Jesus announced
3. Mary visits Elizabeth
4. The birth of John the Baptist
5. Zechariah prophesies and praises God

B. The birth and boyhood of Jesus
1. The birth of Jesus
2. What the angel says
3. What Simeon says
4. What Anna says
5. The boyhood of Jesus

Meeting the Lord

As you run through Luke's Introduction in your mind you will find that you will remember some of the details of each incident. So, as you do (on your own, or with a friend), please take time to thank God for what he is doing, and to worship Jesus for all that he is.

Luke wrote his Gospel not only so that we will *know about* Jesus. He wants us to *meet* him too.

The Luke experiment is an invitation to do just this.

How to help your memory

1. **Make learning visual** by remembering where the events are on the page of your Bible.

2. **Make learning audible** by learning out loud.

3. **Make learning practical** by doing a little every day.

4. **Make learning enjoyable** by using the experiment to help you pray and worship.

Luke's Gospel
Part One: The King

Chapter 3:1 – 9:50

Part One of the Gospel of Luke
begins at the start of chapter 3
because there is a gap of eighteen years
between the end of Luke's Introduction
and chapter 3 verse 1.

Part One is about **Jesus the King**:
we get to meet Jesus and recognise who he is.
Luke has divided everything into three sections.
Each section contains a number
of blocks of five incidents each.

How do we know where a new section begins?

Section One, as we've just seen,
starts at chapter 3:1.

Luke signals the start of **Section Two**
by providing an introduction (see 6:12-16),
which is called
Jesus chooses the twelve apostles.

Luke signals the start of **Section Three**
by providing another introduction (see 9:1-6).
This one is called
Jesus sends out the twelve apostles.

In this way
Luke has shown us the structure
of Part One of his Gospel.

So **Part One: The King** looks like this:

Section One	3:1 – 6:11	Introducing Jesus
Section Two	6:12 – 8:56	Experiencing Jesus
Section Three	9:1-50	Recognising Jesus

Section One: Introducing Jesus
Luke 3:1 – 6:11

In his Introduction Luke has made it very clear that his Gospel is about Jesus. But the last thing we read about is something Jesus said when he was twelve years old. Now it is eighteen years later. In Section One, Luke introduces us to Jesus as an adult and answers two questions: Who is Jesus? And what did his ministry look like?

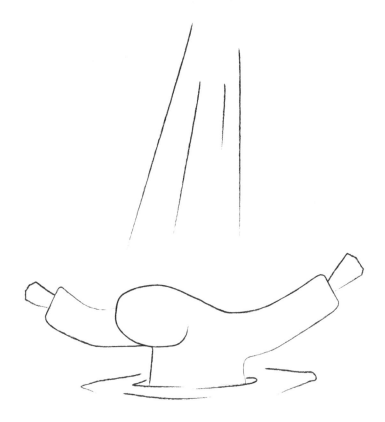

As he was praying, heaven was opened,
and the Holy Spirit descended on him
in bodily form like a dove.
And a voice came from heaven:
'You are my Son, whom I love; with you I am well pleased.'

Luke 3:21-22

Enjoying the View

A. The foundation of Jesus' ministry (3:1 – 4:30)

1. John: his identity and message (3:1-20)
2. Jesus: his baptism (3:21-22)
3. Jesus: his genealogy (3:23-38)
4. Jesus: his temptation (4:1-13)
5. Jesus: his identity and message (4:14-30)

B. The beginning of Jesus' ministry (4:31 – 5:16)

1. Jesus drives out an evil spirit (4:31-37)
2. Jesus heals Simon's mother-in-law and others (4:38-41)
3. Jesus says his priority is preaching (4:42-44)
4. Jesus calls the first disciples (5:1-11)
5. Jesus heals a leper (5:12-16)

C. The opposition to Jesus' ministry (5:17 – 6:11)

1. Jesus forgives and heals a paralysed man (5:17-26)
2. Jesus calls Levi and eats with sinners (5:27-32)
3. Jesus predicts a radical break with Judaism (5:33-39)
4. Jesus is Lord of the Sabbath (6:1-5)
5. Jesus provokes opposition by healing on the Sabbath (6:6-11)

The three blocks in Section One introduce us to the adult Jesus.

Block A lays the foundation: each of its five incidents helps us to see more clearly who Jesus is. And Luke is careful to show us that the ministry of John the Baptist is closely tied to Jesus: he is an essential part of the foundation.

Block B give us five snapshots of Jesus' ministry. After creating a stir in the synagogue in Nazareth at the end of Block A, Jesus preaches and heals more widely in Galilee: and he does it with effortless authority. And a key part of the beginning of Jesus' ministry is his decision to call people to follow him.

Block C brings us a new ingredient: opposition. Now, whenever Jesus is at work, some religious leaders are there. And they don't like what they see: Jesus is doing things which only God should do. And so by the end of the block they have decided to do away with him.

Before reading any further, it would be good to read chapter 3:1 – 6:11 of Luke's Gospel. As you do this, be ready to talk to the Jesus you are reading about and hearing from.

Unpacking the Content

A. The foundation of Jesus' ministry (3:1 – 4:30)

1. – John: his identity and message (3:1-20)

Luke makes it clear that he has not invented what he is about to tell us in his Gospel: he roots it in a specific historical context (see 1-2a).

When we read that *the word of God came to John son of Zechariah* (2b), we should notice that this is a familiar formula which shows that John is really the last of the Old Testament prophets (see Jer 1:1-2, Hos 1:1, Luke 7:26-28).

The prophet Isaiah had said that someone would come as *a voice of one calling in the wilderness, 'Prepare the way for the Lord, make straight paths for him'* (4b, quoting Isa 40:3). And Luke doesn't want us to miss this: he quotes all of verses 3-5 from Isaiah chapter 40.

This is John's identity: he is the forerunner for someone who is God himself.

John communicates three things in his preaching.

First, he calls to repentance (7-9). Luke has already told us that John is *preaching a baptism of repentance for the forgiveness of sins* (3). But now John is calling the people a *brood of vipers* and telling them to *flee from the coming wrath* (7).

Repentance is necessary: no one can be accepted by God because they can say *We have Abraham as our father* (8). Repenting means deciding to give up sin and live in a way that pleases God.

And this is urgent because *every tree that does not produce good fruit will be cut down and thrown into the fire* (9). Judgment is coming, so John's message is clear: *Produce fruit in keeping with repentance* (8).

Second, he gives examples (10-14). It looks like John's preaching is hitting home: Luke tells us that there were *crowds coming out to be baptised* (7). So they ask John what repentance is going to look like in practice.

John explains that *anyone who has two shirts should share with the one who has none* (11). He doesn't tell tax-collectors to stop working for the Romans, but to decide not to *collect any more than you are required to* (13).

And soldiers who come for baptism and ask what repentance should look like for them, are told *Don't extort money and don't accuse people falsely* (14b).

So John is making it clear that repentance needs to be *real.*

Third, he points to the Messiah (15-18). Apparently this preaching is making such an impact that everyone is *wondering in their hearts if John might possibly be the Messiah* (15).

But John points away from himself: someone *more powerful than I will come* [...]. *He will baptise you with the Holy Spirit and fire* (16).

He is talking about the Messiah. In the Old Testament, only God can pour out his Holy Spirit, and John's words here mean that the one he is preparing the way for will usher in the new covenant.

All first-century Jews knew that Scripture promised a new covenant, a new relationship with God (see Jer 31:31-34). This would mean that people were forgiven (see Ezek 36:25-27) and had the Holy Spirit living inside them (see Joel 2:28-32).

John is saying that the time is here: the coming one will bring in the new covenant as he pours out the Holy Spirit.

But he will bring judgment too: yes, he will baptise with the Spirit, but he will also *burn up the chaff with unquenchable fire* (17b, see also 9 and 16b).

Jesus will say it himself later in Luke's Gospel: *I have come to bring fire on the earth* [...]. *Do you think I came to bring peace on earth? No, I tell you, but division* (chapter 12:49a, 51).

John has not told us the name of the Messiah, the one he is preparing the way for. But he has been pointing to him. And in a moment Luke will tell us that *Jesus was baptised* (21). The conclusion is unmistakeable.

In a note at the end of this first incident in Block A, we learn what happened to John because he *rebuked Herod the tetrarch because of his marriage to Herodias, his brother's wife* (19): Herod *locked John up in prison* (20).

But he has done his job. He has prepared the way for Jesus. He has, in Luke's words, *proclaimed the good news* (18b).

2. – Jesus: his baptism (3:21-22)

Before John is thrown into prison he is baptising many people. And now Luke tells us that *Jesus was baptised too* (21). *A baptism of repentance* (3) is for people who admit that they need to get right with God: it looks like Jesus is deliberately identifying with sinners.

This is a hint of what will happen later in the Gospel.

Two things happen as soon as Jesus is baptised.

First, the Spirit comes. *The Holy Spirit descended on him in bodily form like a dove* (22). He is being commissioned for the work he has come to do: it's like God is saying to his Son *Let's save the world!*

Second, the Father speaks. A voice comes from heaven, announcing *You are my Son, whom I love; with you I am well pleased* (22). The message is clear: Jesus is the Father's pride and joy.

As Jesus is baptised, we see all three Persons of the Trinity: the Son in verse 21, the Spirit in verse 22a, and the Father in verse 22b. God himself is intervening dramatically in human affairs.

And Jesus is the Son of God.

3. – Jesus: his genealogy (3:23-38)

The genealogy here differs from the one Matthew provides at the beginning of his Gospel (see Matt 1:1-17): the differences are because Matthew gives us the descendants of David down the *royal* line.

Three things about Jesus are worth picking out here.

First, he's the Son of God (23). Luke reminds us that Jesus *was the son, so it was thought, of Joseph* (23). We know already that Jesus' father is not Joseph, but God himself (see chapter 1:34-35).

Luke is giving us a genealogy traced through Joseph because it was generally assumed that Jesus was his son (see chapter 2:48-50). This establishes Jesus' official place in society.

But don't forget, says Luke: Jesus is the Son of God.

Second, he's descended from David (31). This matters because everyone knew that the saviour God had promised would be a descendant of King David, so much so that the phrase *son of David* was another way of referring to the Messiah.

Third, he's fully human (38). Luke doesn't stop the genealogy when he reaches Abraham in verse 34; instead he goes all the way back to Adam (calling Adam *the son of God* is just another way of saying that God created him).

So Jesus is one of us. And he's come not just for Israel, but for the whole of humankind.

If we put these three ingredients together we see that Jesus the Messiah is both divine and human. He is perfectly equipped to be the Saviour of the world.

4. – Jesus: his temptation (4:1-13)

This account is not here to teach us how to deal with temptation in our own lives. Rather it shows us Jesus being tested as he begins his work.

And it is impossible to read this without thinking of Israel's experience after being rescued from slavery in Egypt. Luke begins by telling us that Jesus *was led by the Spirit into the wilderness* (1) and that he fasted *for forty days* while he was *tempted by the devil* (2): Israel was in the wilderness for forty years.

But what makes this link crystal-clear is that in his encounter with Satan Jesus three times quotes from Deuteronomy chapters 6-8, which are an account of Israel's experience in the wilderness.

And, as we shall see, when Jesus is tested in the wilderness he succeeds where Israel failed.

Luke tells us the three tests the devil throws at Jesus.

First, 'Turn these stones into bread' (3-4). Of course Jesus *was hungry* (2b): this is an obvious temptation for the devil to use to begin his assault.

But there is more here. First-century Jews believed that when the Messiah came he would repeat the manna miracle from the story of Moses and Israel in the wilderness: the reaction to Jesus feeding the 5,000 confirms this (see John 6:14-15).

So this is a temptation to Jesus not only to satisfy his hunger, but also to prove his identity.

But Jesus replies that human beings *shall not live on bread alone, but on every word that comes from the mouth of God* (4). He is quoting from Deuteronomy 8:3, which makes the link with the manna miracle.

And let's notice how Satan begins: *If you are the Son of God...* (3a).

Second, 'Worship me, and I'll give you the world' (5-8). Now the devil shows Jesus *all the kingdoms of the world* (5) and *all their authority and splendour* (6). He is offering him worldwide dominion.

But at a price. Jesus can have all this, says Satan, *if you worship me* (7).

Jesus' mission *was* to be acknowledged by humankind (see Daniel 7:14), but Satan's way for him to achieve this would by-pass the cross. So Jesus again uses the book of Deuteronomy: *Worship the Lord your God, and serve him only* (10b, quoting Deut 6:13).

Third, 'Throw yourself down from the temple' (9-12). For this third temptation, Satan once again asks Jesus to prove his identity: *If you are the Son of God...* (9).

First-century Jews believed that the Messiah would one day stand on the roof of the temple and proclaim the kingdom of God.

But the devil takes this a step further. He explains that Jesus can throw himself off the temple because God *will command his angels concerning you* [...], and *they will lift you up in their hands* (6, quoting Psalm 91:11-12).

Satan is using the Scriptures to entice Jesus to prove his identity again.

For his answer Jesus goes back to the key chapters in Deuteronomy. This time he quotes verse 16 of chapter 6: *Do not put the Lord your God to the test* (7).

So Jesus has passed the test. And Luke tells us that *when the devil had finished all this tempting, he left him until an opportune time* (13).

5. – Jesus: his identity and message (4:14-30)

Luke began Block A by looking at the identity and message of John the Baptist, but very soon the focus turned to Jesus. So the block ends with the identity and message of Jesus himself.

This incident in the synagogue in Nazareth probably happened somewhat later, but Luke brings it up front because it's so important to him: here we have the manifesto with which Jesus begins his ministry.

It tells us how Jesus sees himself.

So Luke gives us a very full account of what happened.

But there is something else in this passage, too. Three times we read how people are responding to Jesus or, more specifically, to his message (see 14-15, 22, 28-30).

It's like Luke is asking us the question *How are you responding to Jesus and his message?*

Jesus' manifesto is divided in two; if we add in the three different responses to him we will see that the passage has five main parts.

First, people's reaction: enthusiasm (14-15). Jesus has returned to Galilee *in the power of the Spirit,* which is what we would expect (14, see also chapter 3:22 and 4:1).

Jesus is doing miracles (see 23b), but Luke doesn't mention them here. Instead he tells us that *he was teaching in their synagogues* (15a).

And the overwhelming reaction to Jesus is enthusiasm: *Everyone praised him* (15b).

Second, Jesus' announcement (16-21). In the synagogue *he stood up to read* (16b). But this is not any synagogue: this is Nazareth, *where he had been brought up* (16a).

These people know him well.

Jesus has probably been invited to read Scripture and speak: they know his reputation. He reads words from the prophecy of Isaiah (chapter 61:1-2) which would have been very familiar to his listeners.

The first sentence sets the tone: *The Spirit of the Lord is on me, because he has anointed me to proclaim good news to the poor* (18a). Jesus reads on: *He has sent me to proclaim freedom for the prisoners and recovery of sight for the blind, to set the oppressed free, to proclaim the year of the Lord's favour* (18b-19).

In this prophecy it's the Messiah who is speaking: he's been *anointed* (18a: *Messiah* means *Anointed One*). What makes that certain is that he's been anointed not with oil by another human being, but with the Spirit, and by God.

What Jesus says next is explosive: *Today this scripture is fulfilled in your hearing* (21).

These are astonishing words. Just as John the Baptist's identity and message were introduced to us with a passage of Old Testament prophecy (see chapter 3:4-6), so now we get the same thing happening with Jesus.

He is unmistakeably claiming to be the Messiah, anointed with the Spirit at his baptism (see chapter 3:22). *He* is the one who will open blind eyes and set people free.

The Jewish people were waiting for the arrival of the Messiah. And now here is Jesus saying *It's me*.

This is Jesus' announcement in the synagogue in Nazareth. How much do his listeners understand, and how is this going to impact them?

Third, people's reaction: puzzlement (22). Everyone is *amazed at the gracious words that came from his lips* (22a). His words are gracious because they are about grace, about what God is going to do in bringing light and freedom into our world.

But there is certainly puzzlement here too. It looks like people can't quite get their heads around this: they're looking at Jesus and asking *Isn't this Joseph's son?* (22b).

Their answer, of course, is *Yes*: how can a carpenter's boy be coming up with stuff like this?

But Luke wants us, his readers, to give a different answer. In the first three chapters of his Gospel an angel, Jesus himself and God the Father have all made clear that Jesus is not *Joseph's* son, but *God's* (see 1:35, 2:49 and 3:22).

But the people in the synagogue in Nazareth are puzzled.

Fourth, Jesus' warning (23-27). He realises that they are going to want to see some miracles before they are willing to believe him. Having said *Physician, heal yourself!* they will tell Jesus to *do here in your home town what we have heard that you did in Capernaum* (23).

Jesus tells everyone in Nazareth's synagogue that he is not surprised by their reaction, because *no prophet is accepted in his home town* (24).

And now comes the warning.

Jesus reminds them that *there were many widows in Israel in Elijah's time.* […] (25). *Yet Elijah was not sent to any of them, but to a widow in Zarephath in the region of Sidon* (26).

To make sure they get the message Jesus gives his listeners another example: *There were many in Israel with leprosy in the time of Elisha the prophet, yet not one of them was cleansed – only Naaman the Syrian* (27).

The warning could not be clearer. Sometimes, when his own people have refused to respond to him, God has not blessed Israel but blessed pagans instead. It's like Jesus is warning everyone that history might just repeat itself.

Fifth, people's reaction: anger (28-30). There are no exceptions: *All the people in the synagogue were furious when they heard this* (28).

Jesus is insulting their nation and so insulting God. He's implying that God loves Gentiles too.

So what do they do? They *drove him out of the town, and took him to the brow of the hill on which the town was built, in order to throw him off the cliff* (29).

They are deciding to do away with Jesus. This is too much for them: as they have listened to this man's announcement and warning, they have moved from puzzlement to anger.

It's like Luke is asking us, his readers, how *we* are going to respond to Jesus.

This theme of Jesus coming for Gentiles as well as Jews will return later in the Gospel, and especially in Section Five.

But the encounter between Jesus and the people of Nazareth is over. The lynch mob don't succeed: Jesus *walked right through the crowd and went on his way* (30).

But before we leave Nazareth, it's worth returning to verse 20. After finishing the reading, Jesus gives the Isaiah scroll back to the attendant, and Luke adds that *the eyes of everyone in the synagogue were fastened on him* (20b).

Why is that?

It could just be that they sense a quiet authority in Jesus which makes them want to hear what he has to say. But it could also be that they know he has stopped reading in the middle of a sentence.

The Isaiah passage tells us that the Messiah comes to proclaim the year of the Lord's favour *and the day of vengeance of our God* (Isa 61:2a).

Jesus has not read out the message of God's coming judgment because he is going to do something which will result in people not having to face that judgment: he will take the punishment for the sins of others on to himself (see, for example, Isa 53:6).

Section One's Block A is done. Luke has given us the foundation of Jesus' ministry: in John the Baptist's summons to baptism and repentance, in God the Father's commissioning of his Son, and in Jesus' faithfulness when tempted by Satan.

And in his commitment, whatever the opposition, to proclaim light for the blind and freedom for the prisoner. And he does this as God's Messiah.

Which is what Jesus goes on to do in Block B.

B. The beginning of Jesus' ministry (4:31 – 5:16)

In his next block of five incidents, Luke gives us an idea of what Jesus' ministry looked like. It seems to be based in Capernaum, a town on the shores of Lake Galilee.

One of the things these five incidents have in common is that Jesus meets no human opposition of any kind: Luke will wait until Block C to show us that the religious leaders don't share the initial enthusiasm of the crowds.

1. – Jesus drives out an evil spirit (4:31-37)

Jesus is in the synagogue in Capernaum, where the people *were amazed at his teaching* (32, compare verses 14-15).

But there's an interruption: *there was a man possessed by a demon* (33), who shouts the question *Have you come to destroy us?* (34). It looks like the forces of evil know that Jesus has authority over them.

They know something else, too. This is not just *Jesus of Nazareth* (34a); this is *the Holy One of God* (34b). This is almost certainly a designation for the Messiah (see John 6:69).

Commanded by Jesus to leave the man, the demon *threw the man down before them all and came out without injuring him* (35).

At the beginning of this incident the people in the synagogue *were amazed at his teaching* (32); now, after Jesus' expulsion of the demon, *all the people were amazed* again (36a). Notice how they describe what has happened: *With authority and power he gives orders to impure spirits and they come out!* (36b).

Jesus is making a name for himself already: *the news about him spread throughout the surrounding area* (37).

2. – Jesus heals Simon's mother-in-law and others (4:38-41)

Jesus has obviously been teaching and healing, but Luke has not said anything about Jesus calling disciples. But clearly he and Simon are already friends, because Simon invites him to his home.

Simon's mother-in-law is *suffering from a high fever* (38); *they asked Jesus to help her* (38b): they know he can heal. The fact that Jesus *rebuked the fever* (39) suggests that it's like he's telling it to go.

So the fever *left her* (39), at which she gets up and looks after her guests.

After the Sabbath is over (*at sunset,* 40a), people bring to Jesus *all who had various kinds of illness, and laying his hands on each one, he healed them* (40). This 100% success rate shows us the authority of Jesus in action again.

It looks like Jesus is driving out demons, too. Not just out of compassion, but in order to prevent them shouting out his identity for all to hear. They call him *the Son of God* (41a), so Jesus rebukes them.

And Luke adds that Jesus *would not allow them to speak, because they knew he was the Messiah* (41b).

The most likely reason for this is that Jewish expectations of a political Messiah who would throw the Romans out of Israel would make life hard for Jesus: it would be difficult to stick to the agenda for his ministry that he had announced in the synagogue in Nazareth (see chapter 4:16-21).

3. – Jesus says his priority is preaching (4:42-44)

Jesus has got up early and gone to a lonely spot (see 42). Mark, in his Gospel, has Simon telling Jesus *Everyone is looking for you!* (Mark 1:37); this is confirmed by Luke who says *the people were looking for him* (42). They want to *keep him from leaving them* (42b).

But Jesus knows that he must move on: *I must proclaim the good news of the kingdom of God to the other towns also* (43).

It looks like this is Jesus' short summary of the message God the Father wants him to preach. It was Israel's hope that one day God would establish his kingship over all people, and this was known as *the kingdom of God.*

And Jesus has already claimed that this is now happening in his ministry (see chapter 4:18-19, and especially 21).

This, says Jesus, *is why I was sent* (43b).

Of course Jesus will also do miracles of healing and exorcism. But his priority is to preach the kingdom of God.

4. – Jesus calls the first disciples (5:1-11)

This may be the same event described for us in Mark 1:16-20, but I'm inclined to think that it isn't.

Luke takes his time to tell the story. And, although others are also being called to be disciples here, the focus is firmly on Simon.

First, what Simon hears (1-3). The *Lake of Gennesaret* (1) is Luke's way of talking about Lake Galilee. And Jesus is the centre of attention: *the people were crowding round him and listening to the word of God* (1b).

Two fishing boats are there *at the water's edge* (2). So Jesus *got into one of the boats, the one belonging to Simon, and asked him to put out a little from the shore* (3a).

This is Jesus' way of making sure that everyone can see and hear him, and that his teaching will be uninterrupted by requests for healings (see Mark 3:9-10 and 4:1).

So, says Luke, Jesus *sat down and taught the people from the boat* (3). People in the crowd can walk away if they want to; but Simon and those with him are a captive audience.

This is what Simon hears: he is listening to Jesus teaching *the word of God* (1b).

Second, what Simon sees (4-7). After *he had finished speaking,* Jesus tells Simon to *put out into deep water, and let down the nets for a catch* (4).

This is a big ask. The best fishing is close to the shore at night, not in deep water during the day. Simon tells Jesus that he and his colleagues (I assume Simon's brother Andrew is among those in the boat with him) have *worked hard all night and haven't caught anything* (5a).

But Simon has seen Jesus in action (see chapter 4:38-41) and has now heard him teaching: he knows enough to be able to call him *Master* (5a). So he tells Jesus that *because you say so, I will let down the nets* (5b).

The result is not that they catch *some* fish: *they caught such a large number of fish that their nets began to break* (6). Simon is seeing something extraordinary. The catch is so huge that *they signalled to their partners in the other boat to come and help them* (7a).

This miracle is immense: they *filled both boats so full that they began to sink* (7b).

Simon is not only seeing the huge catch of fish: he is also seeing that Jesus is someone who can do extraordinary, supernatural things.

What Simon sees is going to change his life for ever.

Third, what Simon feels (8-10a). He and his companions are *astonished at the catch of fish they had taken* (9, and see 10a), and it looks like Simon thinks he has no choice: he *fell at Jesus' knees and said, 'Go away from me, Lord; I am a sinful man!'* (8).

He doesn't care what the others in his boat and in the other boat might think: he *has* to respond like this. And instead of calling Jesus *Master* (5a), he's now calling him *Lord* (8a).

Experiencing this overwhelming example of supernatural power leads to Simon feeling his own sinfulness; and this in turn makes him think that Jesus should have nothing to do with people like him.

Simon feels dirty. And afraid.

Fourth, what Simon does (10b-11). Jesus clearly has no intention of turning away from Simon: he tells him *Don't be afraid* (10b).

And then comes the astonishing statement: *From now on you will fish for people* (10b). This is a promise directed at Simon, but James and John in the other boat (see 7 and 10a) and Simon's brother Andrew in the boat with Simon clearly think that Jesus means them, too.

Luke tells us that *they pulled their boats up on shore, left everything and followed him* (11).

They are four new Jesus disciples. They're not just *leaving* their boats; they are, metaphorically speaking, burning them too.

And these first disciples of Jesus *will fish for people* (10b). Just as Jesus has called Simon and the others, they, in turn, will help many other people to get to know Jesus.

This calling of the first disciples is part of the beginning of Jesus' ministry: he is building a team. And Luke wants to be sure that we, his readers, understand who this Simon is: once in the passage he calls him *Simon Peter* (8a).

There is one more incident in Luke's Block B.

5. – Jesus heals a leper (5:12-16)

A leper falls before Jesus and says *Lord, if you are willing, you can make me clean* (12). The word translated *Lord* may simply mean *Sir*: this man is showing his respect for Jesus.

And his faith too. He is sure that Jesus can heal him of his leprosy if he wants to.

Jesus says to him *I am willing* [...]. *Be clean* (13). But before he does this, he *reached out his hand and touched the man* (13a). This is extraordinary love: Jesus doesn't need to touch in order to heal; but maybe no one has touched this man for years.

So we can only imagine how he feels as Jesus touches him.

Now Luke tells us that *immediately the leprosy left him* (13b). It's not a gradual process, it's an immediate miracle. This is the effortless authority of Jesus.

And let's notice this: Jesus is more infectious than the disease!

But there is more to come. Jesus orders this man *Don't tell anyone, but go, show yourself to the priest and offer the sacrifices that Moses commanded for your cleansing, as a testimony to them* (14).

Jesus is keeping the religious and ceremonial rules: he knows that these things must happen for the man to be readmitted to normal social interaction.

The reason Jesus says *Don't tell anyone* (14a) may be that he doesn't want to be overwhelmed with requests for healings and exorcisms: his priority, as he has already made clear, is to *proclaim the good news of the kingdom of God* (see chapter 4:43).

But of course Jesus is increasingly a major topic of conversation: *News about him spread all the more, so that crowds of people came to hear him and to be healed of their illnesses* (15).

In Block B we have discovered what the beginning of Jesus' ministry looked like. He is teaching and healing as the crowds grow. But, Luke tells us, *Jesus often withdrew to lonely places and prayed* (16).

He is spending time with his Father and learning what the next steps of his ministry are going to look like (see John 8:28, Isa 50:4b).

C. The opposition to Jesus' ministry (5:17 – 6:11)

So far Jesus has not encountered opposition, except in his home town (see chapter 4:28-30). But now, in Block C, in the five incidents Luke recounts, there is opposition every step of the way.

And it comes from the religious elite.

1. – Jesus forgives and heals a paralysed man (5:17-26)

Jesus is teaching, and *Pharisees and teachers of the law were sitting there* (17a). And not just a few of them: *they had come from every village of Galilee and from Judea and Jerusalem* (17b).

So news about Jesus has reached the upper echelons of Jewish religion.

Before the story proper starts Luke goes to the trouble of telling us that *the power of the Lord was with Jesus to heal those who were ill* (17c).

There are so many people in the house listening to Jesus, that when some men want to bring their paralysed friend, they decide to dismantle part of the roof and lower him down *into the middle of the crowd, right in front of Jesus* (19).

This is an expression of their faith, and Jesus sees that (see 20a).

Everyone is thinking that he will say to the man *You are healed; stand up!* But Jesus confounds their expectations by saying *Friend, your sins are forgiven* (20).

Maybe there's a stunned silence. What *is* Jesus doing?

Jesus doesn't mean that this man's paralysis is caused by his sin. Rather he is saying that there is something even more important than physical healing.

Forgiveness.

In the silence the Pharisees and the scribes are thinking hard: *Who is this fellow who speaks blasphemy? Who can forgive sins but God alone?* (21).

They are right. By forgiving the paralysed man's sins Jesus is doing something that only God has the right to do. This is blasphemy.

Unless Jesus is God.

Luke tells us that *Jesus knew what they were thinking* (22a). So he asks the Pharisees and the scribes a question: *Which is easier: to say 'Your sins are forgiven' or to say 'Get up and walk'?* (23).

The question is brilliant.

It's easier to *say* the sentence about forgiveness, because that demands no physical evidence. It's much harder to *say* that a paralysed man should get up and walk, because everyone will see if nothing happens.

So Jesus has said the easier sentence already (the one about forgiveness). When he now says the harder one (about healing), and the paralysed man is healed, that will be the proof that Jesus has also forgiven his sins.

Jesus says to the Pharisees and the scribes *I want you to know that the Son of Man has authority on earth to forgive sins* (24a). Then he turns to the paralysed man and tells him *Get up, take your mat and go home* (24b).

And immediately the man is healed.

It's important that we understand what Jesus has just done: he has healed the paralysed man *and so proved that he has forgiven him too.*

At the end of the story Luke tells us that *everyone was amazed and gave praise to God* (26).

Except that's not true. I don't think the religious elite are impressed by what's happened.

The opposition to Jesus has begun.

2. – Jesus calls Levi and eats with sinners (5:27-32)

Jesus tells a tax collector, who is sitting at his tax booth, to follow him: *Levi got up, left everything and followed him* (28).

When Jesus called Simon, Andrew, James and John to be his disciples, there was no opposition (see chapter 5:1-11).

But things have changed.

Levi decides to hold *a great banquet for Jesus at his house, and a large crowd of tax collectors and others were eating with them* (29). It looks like Levi wants all his friends to meet Jesus.

The guest list is a Guide to the Galilean Underworld, and Jesus.

But some Pharisees and some scribes get wind of what's happening. So they ask Jesus' disciples why they *eat and drink with tax collectors and sinners* (30). Sharing food and drink was a sign of acceptance and welcome, so the religious leaders are not happy.

Jesus answers their question by using a picture: *It is not the healthy who need a doctor, but those who are ill* (31). The tax collectors and sinners are spiritually ill, and Jesus is the doctor who can heal them by offering forgiveness.

Jesus adds that he has *not come to call the righteous* (or those who think that they are), *but sinners to repentance* (32). Which is the same message John the Baptist had preached (see chapter 3:7-9).

The opposition is growing.

3. – Jesus predicts a radical break with Judaism (5:33-39)

The accusation here is that Jesus and his disciples are not fasting the way John the Baptist's disciples do and the disciples of the Pharisees do: *yours go on eating and drinking* (33). Luke doesn't tell us who's doing the accusing, but it may well be the Pharisees and the scribes still.

In reply, Jesus uses three parable-pictures. Each of them points to the rupture that is going to come between Jesus and first-century Jewish religion.

First, the bridegroom (34-35). *Can you make the friends of the bridegroom fast while he is with them?* (34). In the Old Testament it is God who is the bridegroom (see, for example, Hosea 2:16, 19-20), and here Jesus is casting himself in the role.

But one day *the bridegroom will be taken from them; in those days they will fast* (35). Jesus is thinking of the cross: then all who love him will fast and grieve.

Are the Pharisees and the scribes friends of the bridegroom?

Second, the patch (36). You don't repair an old piece of clothing with a patch made of new material, because *the patch from the new will not match the old* (36).

The old piece of clothing is first-century Judaism. But Jesus has not come to patch it up or to repair it: he has come with something new.

Third, the new wine (37-39). If you pour new wine into old wineskins *the new wine will burst the skins* (37).

Jesus is the new wine, while the religious leaders of Judaism are the old wineskins. They are not going to be able to accommodate or contain Jesus and his teaching about the kingdom of God.

So there needs to be a new container for Jesus and his disciples, for *new wine must be poured into new wineskins* (38). Is Jesus thinking of the church?

Jesus finishes by warning that *no one after drinking old wine wants the new, for they say 'The old is better'* (39). The religious leaders of first-century Judaism are content with what they have: they are sure to reject him.

Of course Jesus loves the Pharisees and the scribes: he loves his own people. But there will be a radical break between him and them.

4. – Jesus is Lord of the Sabbath (6:1-5)

Jesus' disciples are picking ears of corn on the Sabbath, so some of the Pharisees ask *Why are you doing what is unlawful on the Sabbath?* (2).

Old Testament Law prohibited harvesting in someone else's field, but said *You may pick the ears with your hands* (Deut 23:25). But as far as the Pharisees are concerned, the disciples are harvesting: they are working on the Sabbath.

Jesus replies by reminding them of an incident when David and his companions were hungry and ate *the consecrated bread,* which is *lawful only for priests to eat* (4). Keeping the rules gave way to human need.

But now Jesus adds something incredibly provocative: *The Son of Man is Lord of the Sabbath* (5).

It is worth mentioning here that the phrase *Son of Man,* which Jesus sometimes uses to identify himself with the glorious Son of Man of Daniel 7:13-14, was also used in the first century as another way of referring to oneself (compare Matt 16:13 with Mark 8:27 for an example of this).

This is what Jesus is doing here: he is saying *I am the Lord of the Sabbath.* Or, in other words, *I can decide what is allowed and not allowed on the Sabbath.*

It is not difficult to imagine how the Pharisees and the scribes feel, when Jesus says this to them.

5. – Jesus provokes opposition by healing on the Sabbath (6:6-11)

Jesus is teaching in the synagogue; there is a man there *whose right hand was shrivelled* (6). So the Pharisees and the scribes *watched him closely to see if he would heal on the Sabbath* (7).

Luke tells us that *Jesus knew what they were thinking* (8a). He tells the man with the shrivelled hand to *get up and stand in front of everyone* (8b).

It looks like Jesus is being deliberately provocative.

Turning to the Pharisees and the scribes, Jesus asks *Which is lawful on the Sabbath: to do good or to do evil, to save life or to destroy it?* (9).

They have no answer. If they reply that it's right to do good on the Sabbath, then they can have no problem with Jesus healing the man.

Jesus tells the man to stretch out his hand – something he could probably never do. Luke tells us that *he did so, and his hand was completely restored* (10).

The last sentence of Block C is chilling: the Pharisees and the scribes *were furious and began to discuss with one another what they might do to Jesus* (11).

With his five incidents in this block Luke has shown us how fierce the opposition is. While Jesus continues to reach out in compassion to suffering people, the religious leaders have already made their decision.

Learning the Gospel

The structure of Section One makes it easy to learn.

Just learn the three headings in bold for the three blocks of five; remember that saying them aloud will make this much easier.

Now learn the titles of the five incidents in Block A. This is easy: the first and the last are about the identity and message of John the Baptist, and then of Jesus. The three ingredients in the middle will lodge in your memory quickly.

As you do this, you will find yourself remembering all kinds of details in Luke's account.

Now do the same with Blocks B and C.

You will find this easier to do if you have arranged with a friend to meet up after you have both learnt Section One.

Learning Section One can be done in about ten minutes. And it's worth it.

Section One: Introducing Jesus

A. The foundation of Jesus' ministry
1. John: his identity and message
2. Jesus: his baptism
3. Jesus: his genealogy
4. Jesus: his temptation
5. Jesus: his identity and message

B. The beginning of Jesus' ministry
1. Jesus drives out an evil spirit
2. Jesus heals Simon's mother-in-law and others
3. Jesus says his priority is preaching
4. Jesus calls the first disciples
5. Jesus heals a leper

C. The opposition to Jesus' ministry
1. Jesus forgives and heals a paralysed man
2. Jesus calls Levi and eats with sinners
3. Jesus predicts a radical break with Judaism
4. Jesus is Lord of the Sabbath
5. Jesus provokes opposition by healing on the Sabbath

Meeting the Lord

Once you have committed the structure to memory, start to tell the events of the section to yourself, or to a friend, including as many details as you remember. As you do this, the Holy Spirit will be using the Jesus story in your life.

This will get you praying and worshipping too.

As you run through Section One's incidents in your mind, take time to thank God that Jesus is the Messiah and the Son of God and that he came to bring light to the blind and freedom for the captives; thank Jesus for his effortless authority in healing and preaching; and thank him for his determination, despite the opposition, to keep proclaiming the kingdom of God.

This is the Luke experiment: as you re-tell Luke you will be rediscovering Jesus.

Section Two: Experiencing Jesus
Luke 6:12 – 8:56

At the end of Section One we saw how the opposition from the religious leaders was growing. Now, at the beginning of Section Two, Jesus chooses twelve of his disciples to be apostles. In the rest of the section he gives them the opportunity to experience him in action as he proclaims the kingdom of God in preaching and in works of power. All of this pushes one question about Jesus to the front of *their* minds and ours: *Who is this man?*

He got up and rebuked the wind and the raging waters;
the storm subsided, and all was calm. […]
In fear and amazement they asked one another,
'Who is this?
He commands even the winds and the water,
and they obey him.'

Luke 8:24b and 25b

Enjoying the View

Introduction: Jesus chooses the twelve apostles (6:12-16)

A. The disciples of Jesus (6:17-49)

1. Blessings and woes (6:20-26)
2. Love your enemies (6:27-36)
3. Don't judge others (6:37-42)
4. A tree and its fruit (6:43-45)
5. The wise and foolish builders (6:46-49)

B. The authority of Jesus (7:1 – 8:3)

1. Jesus heals a centurion's servant (7:1-10)
2. Jesus raises a widow's son from death (7:11-17)
3. Jesus and John the Baptist (7:18-35)
4. Jesus is anointed by a sinful woman (7:36-50)
5. Jesus' team includes many women (8:1-3)

C. The teaching of Jesus (8:4-21)

1. The parable of the sower (8:4-8)
2. Jesus explains why he teaches in parables (8:9-10)
3. Jesus explains the parable of the sower (8:11-15)
4. The parable of the lamp (8:16-18)
5. Jesus' true family (8:19-21)

D. The power of Jesus (8:22-56)

1. Jesus calms a storm (8:22-25)
2. Jesus drives out Legion (8:26-39)
3. Jesus meets Jairus (8:40-42a)
4. Jesus heals a sick woman (8:42b-48)
5. Jesus raises Jairus' daughter from death (8:49-56)

We know that Section Two begins at chapter 6:12 because there's an introduction about the apostles. (We will meet a similar introduction at the beginning of Section Three.) Once again, Luke has structured this section with blocks of five incidents each: this helps the memory.

There are four blocks in Section Two. In Block A Jesus explains how he wants his disciples to live, while in Blocks B, C and D the apostles get to see his authority, hear his teaching and experience his power. In Block D they are already asking themselves about Jesus' identity.

It would be good to read though Luke 6:12 – 8:56 before reading any further in *The Luke Experiment*. Be ready to meet Jesus: it is only a short step from reading to worship.

Unpacking the Content

Introduction: Jesus chooses the twelve apostles (6:12-16)

Of all those who are following him, Jesus is going to choose twelve to be his inner team. Before making the decision he goes up a mountain *and spent the night praying to God* (12): he is asking his Father for direction (see John 8:28 and Isa 50:4b).

Jesus chooses these twelve *whom he designated apostles* (13b): the word means *sent ones.* After they have got to know him and been trained by him, he will send them out as his representatives.

The provocative thing is that Jesus settles on the number twelve. There were twelve patriarchs and twelve tribes of Israel: it looks like Jesus is setting up the leadership structure for the true Israel of the kingdom of God.

The slight differences in the apostle lists in the Gospels are explained by the fact that many Jews had two names: for example, *Matthew* (15) and Levi (see chapter 5:27) are the same person.

The two names that jump out from the list are the first and the last: *Simon (whom he named Peter)* (14) and *Judas Iscariot, who became a traitor* (16).

A. The disciples of Jesus (6:17-49)

We are going to listen to Jesus teaching about how he wants those who follow him to live. But first Luke tells us about the audience.

There is *a large crowd of his disciples* (17a) and *a great number of people from all over Judea, from Jerusalem, and from the coastal region around Tyre and Sidon* (17b).

In other words this is a huge crowd that has come from everywhere. They've come to listen and to be healed.

This is an *event*, says Luke: *the people all tried to touch him, because power was coming from him and healing them all* (19).

But, nevertheless, they are willing to listen.

1. – Blessings and woes (6:20-26)

First, the blessings (20-23). The problem with *blessed* is that we don't use the word in modern English. *Happy* is no better, because that just describes a psychological state. A better translation might be *fortunate* or *enviable*. In other words, if you are like this, it's because God is at work in your life.

It is likely that the characteristics mentioned here are to be understood spiritually (compare Matt 5:3-10).

Blessed are you who are poor, says Jesus (20). This is about recognising our poverty before God: spiritually speaking, we are bankrupt.

Blessed are you who hunger (21a) is talking about being dissatisfied with what this world has to offer, and longing for what God wants to give us.

Blessed are you who weep (21b) because we know that we are not as we should be.

And *blessed are you when people hate you, when they exclude you and insult you* because we belong to Jesus (*because of the Son of Man,* 22).

Second, the woes (24-26). After the four positive characteristics, Jesus now moves on to four negative ones. The word *woe* in the Bible nearly always refers to God's judgment on sin.

Woe to you who are rich (24): if we look for our contentment there, that is all we will get.

Woe to you who are well fed (25a), because we are not going to look for anything from God, and what we have won't last.

Woe to you who laugh (25b), if we think that life is all about enjoying ourselves: one day we will change our minds.

Woe to you when everyone speaks well of you (26) because we're just saying what people want to hear.

Third, the rewards (20-23). Jesus stresses that no one ever loses out by becoming his disciple: God always rewards faithfulness.

The rewards involve knowing that we are accepted by God (see 20b), and experiencing real satisfaction and joy (see 21). We will be people who *flourish*.

Jesus sums it up by telling disciples that *great is your reward in heaven* (23).

This is what Jesus wants his disciples to look like. And if we increasingly live like this, we are *blessed*: we are to be envied because God is at work in our lives.

2. – Love your enemies (6:27-36)

Jesus' disciples are to actively love those who hate, curse and ill-treat them: they are to do good to their enemies, bless them and pray for them (see 27-28).

This applies to violence: *If someone slaps you on one cheek, turn to them the other also* (29a); and to theft: *If someone takes your coat, do not withhold your shirt from them* (29b).

It's worth remembering that this is in the context of persecution (see 22).

Jesus sums up his message: *Do to others as you would have them do to you* (31). Such teaching is common in other ethical systems, but there it's nearly always negative (ie *Don't do to others what you wouldn't like others to do to you*).

Jesus is not looking for non-hate in his disciples: he's looking for *love*.

It's easy to love our friends, but Jesus says *If you love those who love you, what credit is that to you?* (32a). So he says it again: *Love your enemies* (35a).

If Jesus' disciples commit themselves to loving their enemies, their reward *will be great* (35) and they will be seen to be *children of the Most High, because he is kind to the ungrateful and wicked* (35b).

Jesus is not saying this is easy. But everyone who has come to know him will want to *be merciful, just as your Father is merciful* (36).

3. – Don't judge others (6:37-42)

Jesus teaches a principle here: *With the measure you use, it will be measured to you* (38b).

This works in negative things: *Do not judge,* says Jesus (37). The word is ambiguous: what is being condemned is self-righteous fault-finding. *Do not condemn* uses a different word to say the same thing (37).

And it works in positive things too: *Forgive, and you will be forgiven. Give, and it will be given to you* (37b-38a).

So we are not to big ourselves up and think we're better than we are: *Can the blind lead the blind? Will they not both fall into a pit?* (39).

And Jesus' description of a funny situation makes this clear: *Why do you look at the speck of sawdust in your brother's eye and pay no attention to the plank in your own eye?* (41). Instead of just a larger piece of sawdust, it's a plank!

In other words, it's ridiculous to write others off when we are far from perfect ourselves.

4. – A tree and its fruit (6:43-45)

This is Jesus using another parable. Just as *each tree is recognised by its own fruit* (44a), you can tell what someone's heart is like by looking at what they do.

So *a good man brings good things out of the good stored up in his heart, and an evil man brings evil things out of the evil stored up in his heart* (45a).

It's obvious, when you come to think of it.

Jesus seems to be telling us to go deeper. It's not just a matter of behaviour, though of course that's important. It's about the state of our hearts.

And the only one who can do something about that is God.

Jesus has one more thing to say to round off his teaching about discipleship.

5. – The wise and foolish builders (6:46-49)

This parable has a very similar lesson. Jesus asks *Why do you call me 'Lord, Lord,' and do not do what I say?* (46).

It's all about the foundation of our lives, about what we're building our lives on.

There are two men, each building a house: but the foundations are very different. One *dug down deep and laid the foundation on rock* (48a), while the other *built a house on the ground without a foundation* (49).

When the storm comes on the first builder's house, *the torrent [...] could not shake it* (48b), while the second builder's *collapsed and its destruction was complete* (49b).

Jesus spells out his message. Either we are someone *who comes to me and hears my words and puts them into practice* (47), or we are a person *who hears my words and does not put them into practice* (49a).

The only firm foundation for our lives is a determination to listen to Jesus *and to obey him.*

Jesus' teaching in Block A is not just for the apostles; it's for everyone who wants to follow Jesus (see 20a). It answers an important question: When people make the decision to follow Jesus and come into the kingdom of God, what will they look like? How does being a Jesus disciple change someone?

Now Luke moves on to Section Two's Block B.

B. The authority of Jesus (7:1 – 8:3)

1. – Jesus heals a centurion's servant (7:1-10)

In Capernaum *a centurion's servant, whom his master valued highly, was ill and about to die* (2). So this man doesn't think his servant is worthless: he values him.

The Roman centurion has *sent some elders of the Jews* to Jesus (3) with his request for healing. They are absolutely on his side: they tell Jesus *This man deserves to have you do this, because he loves our nation and has built our synagogue* (4b-5).

It's unlikely that a centurion would have the resources to finance a public building; perhaps he had got some of his soldiers involved in the building work.

But the most important thing about this man is that he's a Gentile. And yet Luke tells us that Jesus *went with them* (6a).

The centurion shows himself to be humble. While Jesus is still on the way he sends a message: *Lord, don't trouble yourself, for I do not deserve to have you come under my roof* (6). Which is why he had asked friends to come to Jesus with his request for help in the first place: *That is why I did not even consider myself worthy to come to you* (7a).

And now he says something extraordinary: *But say the word, and my servant will be healed* (7b).

This is faith.

The centurion explains his thinking: *For I myself am a man under authority, with soldiers under me. I tell this one 'Go', and he goes; and that one 'Come', and he comes. I say to my servant 'Do this', and he does it* (8).

Jesus is astonished: this man is a Gentile. He tells the crowd that *I have not found such great faith even in Israel* (9).

Luke tells us matter-of-factly that *the men who had been sent returned to the house and found the servant well* (10). Once again we see it: Jesus has effortless authority.

Two things are worth adding.

First, in the temple Simeon had said Jesus was *a light for revelation to the Gentiles* (chapter 2:32): now a Roman centurion is demonstrating faith in

Jesus. The topic of Jews and Gentiles in the kingdom of God will be a major issue in Section Five of the Gospel.

And second, whatever else the centurion had heard about Jesus, he knew that he had authority.

Which meant that trusting Jesus was the obvious thing to do. *Even though he never met him.*

2. – Jesus raises a widow's son from death (7:11-17)

Luke is going to show us that Jesus even has authority over death.

He's approaching a town called Nain with *his disciples and a large crowd* (11), only to meet another large crowd coming in the other direction (see 12b).

The reason is that *a dead person was being carried out – the only son of his mother, and she was a widow* (12). She is weeping, grieving the loss of her son and doubtless wondering, too, how she is going to be able to support herself in the future.

When Jesus sees her, *his heart went out to her and he said 'Don't cry'* (13). Jesus is filled with compassion: without being asked, he is going to do something extraordinary.

He goes over and says *Young man, I say to you, get up!* (14). Luke tells us that *the dead man sat up and began to talk* (15a).

This is the authority of Jesus in action: when he speaks to dead people they obey him.

So Jesus *gave him back to his mother* (15b).

Luke tells us that *they were all filled with awe* (16a): we should be too. And they're praising God: *A great prophet has appeared among us. […] God has come to help his people* (16).

They don't mean that Jesus is God, but that in Jesus the presence of God is powerfully at work. But from what we have read so far in his Gospel, Luke must surely want us to see the fuller meaning in what they say.

Jesus *is* God visiting his people.

With authority like this, it's no wonder that *this news about Jesus spread throughout Judea and the surrounding country* (17).

3. – Jesus and John the Baptist (7:18-35)

We have already seen how important John the Baptist was as preparation for the coming of Jesus (see chapter 1:17 and 76; 3:3-6).

Now Jesus teaches about this, because John has sent him a message.

In verses 18-35 Jesus deals with three questions.

First, a question about Jesus (18-23). This is a question asked by John the Baptist, who has been in prison since chapter 3:20. It looks like he has been sure, ever since baptising Jesus, that he is the Messiah (see chapter 3:15-16).

But now he is having doubts.

So he sends some of his disciples to ask Jesus the question *Are you the one who is to come, or should we expect someone else?* (20).

John may be wondering if Jesus is the real thing because he remembers words from the Messiah's manifesto in the prophecy of Isaiah. He will not have been in the synagogue in Nazareth to hear Jesus quoting this (see chapter 4:16-19), but he will have known these words nevertheless.

They begin like this: *The Spirit of the Sovereign Lord is on me, because the Lord has anointed me to proclaim good news to the poor* (Isa 61:1a).

But look at what follows: *He has sent me to bind up the broken-hearted, to proclaim freedom for the captives and release from darkness for the prisoners* (Isa 61:1b).

Freedom for the captives and the prisoners? John is *in prison.*

Jesus' response is to send a message back to John with a reminder of what is happening in his ministry: *the blind receive sight, the lame walk, those who have leprosy are cleansed, the deaf hear, the dead are raised, and the good news is proclaimed to the poor* (22).

And he adds an encouragement to John to keep trusting him: *Blessed is anyone who does not stumble on account of me* (23).

With his answer to John, Jesus is making it very clear that he really is the Messiah.

Second, a question about John (24-30). Now Jesus asks the crowd a question about John the Baptist and his preaching: *What did you go out into the wilderness to see?* (24).

Jesus provides some wrong answers to the question: *a reed swayed by the wind* (24b) and *a man dressed in fine clothes* (25).

His third answer is right, but it doesn't go far enough: *A prophet? Yes, I tell you, and more than a prophet* (26). By this Jesus probably means that John is the greatest of the prophets because he fulfils God's words to the

Messiah through Malachi: *I will send my messenger ahead of you, who will prepare your way before you* (27, quoting Mal 3:1).

In other words Jesus is saying that John is the forerunner for the Messiah.

This means that there is *no one greater than John* (28a). Yet John himself, says Jesus, preached about the kingdom's arrival but did not experience its reality, with the result that *the one who is least in the kingdom of God is greater than he* (28b).

In answering his own question about John, Jesus has once again made something very clear: he is the Messiah.

In an aside, Luke tells us that *all the people, even the tax collectors, acknowledged that God's way was right* (29a). The reason is that many of them had repented: *they had been baptised by John* (29b).

The religious authorities, on the other hand, *had not been baptised by John* (30b) because they saw no need to repent: the result was that *the Pharisees and the experts in the law rejected God's purpose for themselves* (30a).

In other words: what decides someone's response to God's message is whether they are willing to repent.

But Jesus has a last question to answer.

Third, a question about the crowds (31-35). This third question is asked by Jesus, too: *To what, then, can I compare the people of this generation?* (31).

Using a picture of children playing a game of weddings and funerals (see 32), Jesus says that the crowds, for the most part, are never satisfied. John the Baptist's asceticism and his message of judgment resulted in accusations of demon possession (see 33), while Jesus' time spent with tax collectors and sinners got him labelled *a glutton and a drunkard* (34).

In other words: there is no pleasing these people.

But wisdom, says Jesus, *is proved right by all her children* (35). And the surprising thing, as Luke has told us in verses 29 and 30, is that it is the ordinary people who are wisdom's children, and not the religious elite.

Now we are going to learn that Jesus has authority when speaking about the most important topic of all: forgiveness.

4. – Jesus is anointed by a sinful woman (7:36-50)

This story, which only Luke records for us, is here for a reason: it points us to the authority of Jesus.

First, Jesus is the prophet (36-40). A Pharisee called Simon has invited Jesus for dinner. While they are eating, a woman *who lived a sinful life* comes in, bringing with her *an alabaster jar of perfume* (37). She is probably a town prostitute.

She stands behind Jesus, weeping, and begins *to wet his feet with her tears* (38a). Luke adds that *she wiped them with her hair, kissed them and poured perfume on them* (38b).

And Jesus lets it all happen.

Simon is not impressed. He doesn't say anything, but he's thinking *If this man were a prophet, he would know who is touching him and what kind of woman she is – that she is a sinner* (39b).

But Jesus shows that he is a prophet after all. Luke tells us that *Jesus answered him* (40a): in other words, he knows what Simon is thinking.

When Jesus tells him that he has *something to tell you,* Simon replies *Tell me, teacher* (40b).

Which leads us to the next part of the story.

Second, Jesus is the teacher (41-47). The parable Jesus tells is about two people who owe money: one owes *five hundred denarii, the other fifty* (41). Since neither can pay, the money-lender *forgave the debts of both* (42a).

Then Jesus asks his question: *Which of them will love him more?* (42b).

Simon gives the obvious answer: *I suppose the one who had the bigger debt forgiven* (43a).

Now Jesus draws a comparison between Simon and the woman, showing that the woman has shown him more love than Simon.

Simon didn't provide water for Jesus' feet to be washed, or give him a welcoming kiss, or put olive oil on his head (see 44-46); the woman, on the other hand, *wet my feet with her tears and wiped them with her hair* (44), *has not stopped kissing my feet* (45), and *has poured perfume on my feet* (46).

Now comes the punchline.

Jesus tells Simon that the woman's *many sins have been forgiven – as her great love has shown* (47a). And he ends with a statement about Simon: *Whoever has been forgiven little loves little* (47b).

Jesus the teacher's message is clear: this woman's love for him is not the *basis* of her forgiveness, but the *evidence* for it.

In other words, because the woman already knew that she'd been forgiven (it must surely be that she had met Jesus before), she showed him great love.

Which brings us to the last part of the story.

Third, Jesus is the forgiver (48-50). Jesus wants the woman to know that she is no longer guilty before God: *Your sins are forgiven* (48, a better translation would be *Your sins have been forgiven*).

And he adds: *Your faith has saved you; go in peace* (50).

We don't know if Simon the Pharisee has got the message. But the other dinner guests certainly have: they are asking one another *Who is this who even forgives sins?* (49).

In Section One we heard Jesus claim that *the Son of Man has authority on earth to forgive sins* (see chapter 5:24a). Here in Section Two's Block B he has done it again: he can give people the forgiveness they need.

Jesus has the authority to forgive sin. And when he does, the result is there for all to see.

Luke has one more incident for us, to bring the block to a close.

5. – Jesus' team includes many women (8:1-3)

Jesus *travelled about from one town and village to another, proclaiming the good news of the kingdom of God* (1): he has already made clear that this is his priority (see chapter 4:43a).

Jesus is not alone, of course: *the Twelve were with him* (1b). He has been calling disciples and they have responded to his authority.

But now, instead of referring to the crowds who were following Jesus (see chapter 6:17 and 7:11), Luke tells us that there were also *some women who had been cured of evil spirits and diseases* (2a).

He mentions three by name: Mary Magdalene, *from whom seven demons had come out* (2b), Joanna *the wife of Chuza, the manager of Herod's household* (3a), and Susanna (3a).

And then Luke adds *and many others* (3).

There are two noteworthy things about this.

First, *these women were helping to support them out of their own means* (3b).

And second, the presence of many women among Jesus' travelling companions will have been a potential cause for scandal in first-century Jewish society.

But Luke wants us to know that there were many women in the Jesus team.

C. The teaching of Jesus (8:4-21)

Teaching was a major part of what Jesus was doing in Section One (see 4:15, 31, 43; 5:1, 17; 6:6). But now that he has called the twelve apostles at the beginning of Section Two, it's important that they hear what he has to say.

So in Block C Jesus teaches about the word of God.

The apostles are listening; but there's *a large crowd* there too (4).

1. – The parable of the sower (8:4-8)

As a farmer sows his seed, says Jesus, it falls in different places: *along the path; it was trampled on, and the birds ate it up* (5), on *rocky ground, and when it came up, the plants withered because they had no moisture* (6), *among thorns, which grew up with it and choked the plants* (7) and *on good soil, which yielded a crop, a hundred times more than was sown* (8).

If we were reading this parable for the first time, would we understand its meaning?

There is one clue.

At the end of the story Jesus calls out *Whoever has ears to hear, let them hear* (8b). Could the parable be about how we listen to Jesus teaching the word of God?

2. – Jesus explains why he teaches in parables (8:9-10)

The disciples ask Jesus for the meaning of the story he's told. But first, he explains *why* he uses parables at all.

The reason, says Jesus, is that *the knowledge of the secrets of the kingdom of God has been given to you, but to others I speak in parables* (10). So there are two groups of people: some who don't understand and so reject God's message, and others who may not understand but who ask Jesus to help them (see verse 9).

So the parables are not an intelligence test but an openness test, designed to show to which group each listener belongs. Spiritually open people are hungry to know more and so ask Jesus for help. This is still true today.

Jesus quotes from the Old Testament prophet Isaiah to show that it has always been God's will to hide the message from those who are not open, so that *though seeing, they may not see; though hearing, they may not understand* (10b, quoting Isaiah 6:9).

And now Jesus answers the disciples' question.

3. – Jesus explains the parable of the sower (8:11-15)

The seed is *the word of God* (11), and the four different places where the seed lands are four different kinds of human heart.

So there are hard hearts, where *the devil comes and takes away the word* (12); there are superficial hearts, when after initial enthusiasm people reject the message because *they have no root* (13); there are overfull hearts, where they *are choked by life's worries, riches and pleasures* (14).

And then there are open hearts, which refers to *those with a noble and good heart, who hear the word, retain it, and by persevering produce a crop* (15).

The parable of the sower explains to disciples that what matters is how we listen to the word of God as it is taught by Jesus.

And, when we don't understand, we can ask him for help, as the disciples do here in verse 9.

4. – The parable of the lamp (8:16-18)

You don't hide a lamp, says Jesus; rather you *put it on a stand, so that those who come in can see the light* (16).

The word of God is like that lamp: it needs to be proclaimed (see chapter 4:43), so that everyone can hear it. This is important because God uncovers our secret thoughts and deeds: *there is nothing hidden that will not be disclosed, and nothing concealed that will not be known or brought out into the open* (17).

This is what the word of God does (see also Heb 4:12).

Because of this, says Jesus, *consider carefully how you listen* (18a). And he goes on to give two examples.

First, *whoever has will be given more* (18b): if I am responding to what I have grasped from the word of God I will find myself understanding more and more.

But second, *whoever does not have, even what they think they have will be taken from them* (18c). If I think I know it all, when I have never really started responding to the word of God, I will understand less and less.

The principle is simple: Light received brings more light, but light rejected brings night.

No wonder Jesus tells us to *consider carefully how you listen* (18a).

5. – Jesus' true family (8:19-21)

At first sight it might not look as if this is about the teaching of Jesus. But it is.

Luke tells us that *Jesus' mother and brothers came to see him* (19), but can't get near because of the crowd. (Jesus' sisters are not mentioned: they are still living in Nazareth.)

Told that his family wants to see him, Jesus defines what his true family is: *My mother and brothers are those who hear God's word and put it into practice* (21).

Jesus isn't rejecting his physical family, but he is building a new family. And, as Jesus explained at the end of his teaching in Block A of this section, his team consists of *everyone who comes to me and hears my words and puts them into practice* (chapter 6:47).

Which is exactly what he says here at the end of Block C. When Jesus teaches the word of God, it's not just for hearing.

It's for *doing*, too.

Luke has one more block for us in Section Two.

D. The power of Jesus (8:22-56)

Luke has collected four miracles here, which show that Jesus has limitless power. And they are not random: they show that Jesus is Lord over nature (see 22-25), evil (see 26-39), sickness (see 42b-48) and death (see 49-56).

1. – Jesus calms a storm (8:22-25)

When Jesus says to the disciples *Let us go over to the other side of the lake* (22), they get into a boat and set off, taking Jesus with them.

Luke tells us that *he fell asleep* (23a).

Then something happens which takes them by surprise: *A squall came down on the lake, so that the boat was being swamped, and they were in great danger* (23b).

The disciples wake Jesus and say *Master, Master, we're going to drown!* (24a).

What Luke writes next is astonishing: *He got up and rebuked the wind and the raging waters; the storm subsided, and all was calm* (25). Jesus speaks to the weather, and it looks like the result is immediate: no wind, no waves.

Having spoken to the weather, Jesus now asks his disciples *Where is your faith?* (25a).

It's almost like Jesus is the one who is surprised now. Instead of trusting him, the disciples are prisoners of *fear and amazement* (25b): they are more afraid *after* the storm than they were *during* the storm.

Because they're all asking a question: *Who is this? He commands even the winds and the water, and they obey him* (25c). They don't know the answer yet, but they're asking the right question.

This is the question Luke wants us to be asking ourselves, too.

The storm has obeyed Jesus. He is Lord over nature.

2. – Jesus drives out Legion (8:26-39)

The boat arrives at the other side of Lake Galilee. But at once Jesus is confronted with the powers of evil: *When Jesus stepped ashore, he was met by a demon-possessed man from the town* (27a).

The man is naked and lives in the tombs (see 27b); *though he was chained hand and foot and kept under guard, he had broken his chains and had been driven by the demon into solitary places* (29b).

As soon as he sees Jesus, he falls at his feet and shouts at the top of his voice *What do you want with me, Jesus, Son of the Most High God? I beg you, don't torture me!* (28).

And, when Jesus asks him for his name, the demons, speaking through the man, reply *Legion*: Luke explains that *many demons had gone into him* (30).

Two things are worth noting here.

First, the possessed man recognises Jesus: *Son of the Most High God* may be a way of saying *Messiah.* The disciples don't yet know who Jesus is, but the powers of evil are in no doubt.

And second, the demons acknowledge that Jesus has authority over them. They know he can torture them by commanding them to leave the man. And *they begged Jesus repeatedly not to order them to go into the Abyss* (31).

There are pigs on the hillside and *the demons begged Jesus to let them go into the pigs* (32): it looks like they know Jesus is going to set the man free. And Luke writes: *He gave them permission* (32b).

Sure enough, the demons come out of the man and go into the pigs: *the herd rushed down the steep bank into the lake and was drowned* (33).

But the drama is not over.

The pig-farmers run and tell others; word spreads and people come to see for themselves: *they found the man from whom the demons had gone out, sitting at Jesus' feet, dressed and in his right mind* (35b).

And Luke tells us that *they were afraid* (35c).

This man Jesus is not safe to have around. If he has done this extraordinary miracle, what else might he be capable of?

The result is that *all the people of the region of the Gerasenes asked Jesus to leave them* (37a). They don't want this man anywhere near them.

Before Jesus leaves (see 37b), the man he's set free *begged to go with him* (38). But Jesus has other plans.

He tells the man to go home and *tell how much <u>God</u> has done for you* (39a). And the man, says Luke, goes away and *told all over the town how much <u>Jesus</u> had done for him* (39b).

Do you see how the man changes the message? I don't think he's doing it deliberately, but I'm sure Luke wants us to notice what the man says: he wants us to realise that Jesus is God.

It's the answer to the disciples' question back in verse 25b.

So we've watched as the demons have obeyed Jesus. He is Lord over evil.

3. – Jesus meets Jairus (8:40-42a)

When the boat reaches shore again, someone runs up to Jesus to ask for help: it's *Jairus, a synagogue leader* (41a). He falls at Jesus' feet, *pleading with him to come to his house because his only daughter, a girl of about twelve, was dying* (41b-42a).

The fact that Luke tells us that Jairus is the leader of a synagogue is significant. He may not be a Pharisee or a scribe, but he is a man others look up to.

And Jesus goes with him (see 42b).

4. – Jesus heals a sick woman (8:42b-48)

As Jesus is on his way to Jairus' house, *the crowds almost crushed him* (42b). It looks like everyone wants to be near Jesus.

Luke tells us that *a woman was there who had been subject to bleeding for twelve years* (43). So she is sick, ritually unclean and lonely.

Somehow she manages to come up behind Jesus and touch the edge of his cloak. And something extraordinary happens: *immediately her bleeding stopped* (44b).

The woman knows that she has been *instantly healed* (47b).

It looks like Jesus stops in order to ask a question: *Who touched me?* (45a). My guess is that Jesus really doesn't know the answer. But when Peter explains that everyone is touching him (see 45b), Jesus is adamant: *Someone touched me; I know that power has gone out from me* (46).

At this, the woman *came trembling and fell at his feet* (47). After Jesus has listened to her story (see 47b), he tells her *Daughter, your faith has healed you. Go in peace* (48).

This is a remarkable miracle. Jesus has healed this woman, without deliberately setting out to do so. There is just so much power in this man.

The woman's appalling medical condition obeys Jesus. He is Lord over sickness.

And now we reach the climax of Section Two's Block D.

5. – Jesus raises Jairus' daughter from death (8:49-56)

A messenger from Jairus' house arrives with a message for him: *Your daughter is dead [...]. Don't bother the teacher anymore* (49).

But Jesus is not to be put off. He tells Jairus *Don't be afraid; just believe, and she will be healed* (50).

When Jesus arrives, he takes only the child's parents and Peter, James and John into the house: everyone else is to stay outside (see 51). But as Jesus goes inside he tells *all the people* to stop their wailing (52). And he tells them *why*: *She is not dead but asleep* (52b).

The reaction is inevitable: *They laughed at him, knowing that she was dead* (53).

And then comes the miracle. Now inside the house, Jesus takes the girl by the hand and says *My child, get up!* (54).

Luke tells us matter-of-factly that *her spirit returned, and at once she stood up* (55a). Jairus and his wife are *astonished* (56a), which is probably putting it mildly: we need to try to imagine how they are feeling.

And then Jesus *ordered them not to tell anyone what had happened* (56b). Why does he do that?

Surely it can't be that they were to keep it quiet that the dead girl was now alive: it would be impossible to prevent such astonishing news getting out.

My guess is that Jesus wants them not to say anything as long as he is still in the house: if Jairus leant out of the window and shouted *Jesus has raised her to life!* it would be impossible for Jesus to move on to another place. There would be a riot or something similar.

Whatever the reason Jesus says this, we have seen that death obeys him. Jesus is Lord over death.

Block D has shown us that Jesus is Lord: over nature, over evil, over sickness and over death. It's like Luke is saying to us *Would you like to mention any other area of life?*

The message is clear. If Jesus is Lord over nature, evil, sickness and death, then he is Lord everywhere.

Perhaps this is a good moment for us to ask ourselves if we are willing for him to be Lord over us.

Learning the Gospel

I hope you will take time to learn Section Two. Remember that this is not about learning every word but the order of the events.

First, learn the headings of the four blocks: they are in bold.

When you have mastered the headings in bold, go to Block A and learn the names of the five incidents. This is not difficult if you do it out loud; and as you learn them, many of the details will come back to you.

Then do the same with Block B. And so on.

Remember that it might help to agree with a friend that you will both learn the structure of Section Two. Remember, too, that as more and more of the section gets into your memory, the Holy Spirit will use it to *change* you.

There is power in the word of God.

Section Two: Experiencing Jesus

Introduction: Jesus chooses the twelve apostles

A. The disciples of Jesus
  1. Blessings and woes
  2. Love your enemies
  3. Don't judge others
  4. A tree and its fruit
  5. The wise and foolish builders

B. The authority of Jesus
  1. Jesus heals a centurion's servant
  2. Jesus raises a widow's son from death
  3. Jesus and John the Baptist
  4. Jesus is anointed by a sinful woman
  5. Jesus' team includes many women

C. The teaching of Jesus
  1. The parable of the sower
  2. Jesus explains why he teaches in parables
  3. Jesus explains the parable of the sower
  4. The parable of the lamp
  5. Jesus' true family

D. The power of Jesus
  1. Jesus calms a storm
  2. Jesus drives out Legion
  3. Jesus meets Jairus
  4. Jesus heals a sick woman
  5. Jesus raises Jairus' daughter from death

Meeting the Lord

As you move through the ingredients of Section Two in your mind, tell yourself the story (with as many details as you can remember), or do this with a friend. As you do, keep responding to what you have been thinking by talking to Jesus.

In Block A you will be reminded of how Jesus wants his disciples to live: pray that by his Spirit he will make you more and more like this. As you go through Block B in your mind, thank Jesus for his authority. In Block C ask Jesus to help you to respond to him as he teaches you in his word.

And in Block D worship Jesus for his power and commit yourself to living under his lordship.

One of the main reasons God has given us Luke's Gospel is so that we can encounter Jesus.

He is waiting to meet you.

Section Three: Recognising Jesus
Luke 9:1-50

In Section Two we saw, with the apostles and the crowds, how Jesus was proclaiming the good news of the kingdom of God in his teaching and his miracles. Now, after sending out the apostles on a mission at the beginning of Section Three, Jesus helps them to realise who he is and (at least to hear) why he has come. Every disciple needs to recognise Jesus and to understand why God sent him into the world.

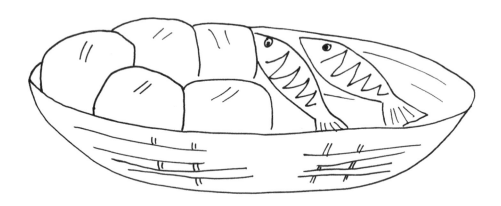

They all ate
and were satisfied...

Luke 9:17a

Enjoying the View

Introduction: Jesus sends out the twelve apostles (9:1-6)

A. Jesus is the Messiah (9:7-27)

1. Herod: his question (9:7-9)
2. Jesus feeds the 5,000 (9:10-17)
3. Peter's confession of Jesus (9:18-21)
4. First prediction (9:22)
5. Jesus: the call to discipleship (9:23-27)

B. Jesus is the Son (9:28-50)

1. The transfiguration (9:28-36)
2. Jesus drives out an evil spirit (9:37-43a)
3. Second prediction (9:43b-45)
4. "I am the greatest" (9:46-48)
5. "We're the only ones" (9:49-50)

We know that Section Three starts at the beginning of chapter 9 because there's an introduction about the apostles. (We saw a similar introduction at the beginning of Section Two.)

Section Three is short: it marks the climax of Part One of Luke's Gospel, as the apostles recognise more clearly who Jesus is.

In Block A the focus is on Jesus being the Messiah, while at the beginning of Block B we learn that he is God's Son.

As we would expect, Luke has structured the section with blocks of five incidents each: this is a help for the memory.

Before reading any further in this book, please read Section Three in Luke's. As you do so, stop from time to time, to ask Jesus questions that occur to you, and to thank him that he is the Messiah and the Son of God.

And please be expecting the Holy Spirit to be using what you read in your life: the word of God *changes* us.

Unpacking the Content

Introduction: Jesus sends out the twelve apostles (9:1-6)

Jesus gives the apostles *power and authority to drive out all demons and to cure diseases* (1). He can do that.

But that's not all. He also *sent them out to proclaim the kingdom of God and to heal those who were ill* (2).

They have seen Jesus doing these things in Section Two; now it is time for them to put it into practice.

But Jesus is clear: they are to *take nothing for the journey* (3a), which will presumably force them to trust God to meet all their needs. Once they have found someone willing to take them in, they are not to move on because they get a better offer, so *whatever house you enter, stay there until you leave that town* (4).

But proclaiming the kingdom of God will have a judgment aspect to it too: *If people do not welcome you, leave their town and shake the dust off your feet as a testimony against them* (5).

This is a huge moment for the apostles: they go *from village to village, proclaiming the good news and healing people everywhere* (6).

A. Jesus is the Messiah (9:7-27)

1. – Herod: his question (9:7-9)

Luke tells us that *Herod the tetrarch heard about all that was going on* (7a): perhaps he has even heard that this Jesus is sending out representatives.

So he has a question: *Who, then, is this I hear such things about?* (9b).

Herod is puzzled, because *some were saying that John had been raised from the dead* (7b), while others plumped for Elijah or another Old Testament prophet.

Herod is not inclined to believe that this is John the Baptist, because he had *beheaded John* (9a). Hence his question: *Who, then, is this I hear such things about?* (9b).

Herod is determined to find out who Jesus is. So, says Luke, *he tried to see him* (9c). His wish will be granted in Part Three of the Gospel (see chapter 23:8-11).

2. – Jesus feeds the 5,000 (9:10-17)

The apostles are back from their mission and are probably tired; so Jesus *took them with him and they withdrew by themselves to a town called Bethsaida* (10b), or probably to the countryside nearby.

When the crowds track Jesus down, *he welcomed them and spoke to them about the kingdom of God* (11). That is, after all, why he had come (see chapter 4:43).

By late in the afternoon the people are hungry, so the disciples tell Jesus to *send the crowd away* (12). But he replies *You give them something to eat* (13a).

Luke tells us that *about five thousand men were there* (14a). Because of this some commentators estimate that, with women and children added into the equation, this might have been a crowd of some 20,000 people.

If it had been, I think Luke would have told us.

When John tells us about this incident in his Gospel, he explains that *the Jewish Passover Festival was near* (John 6:4). This means that almost every adult male was on his way to Jerusalem. So it makes sense to say that this crowd consisted almost exclusively of around 5,000 men.

This is the only miracle of Jesus reported by all four Gospel-writers. What is so important about the feeding of a huge crowd?

Part of the answer may be in an Old Testament prophecy. In a poetic description of what we might call heaven, Isaiah writes: *On this mountain the Lord Almighty will prepare a feast of rich food for all peoples, a banquet of aged wine – the best of meats and the finest of wines. On this mountain he will destroy the shroud that enfolds all peoples, the sheet that covers all nations; he will swallow up death for ever. The Sovereign Lord will wipe away the tears from all faces; he will remove his people's disgrace from all the earth. The Lord has spoken* (Isa 25:6-8).

In the first century Jews referred to this celebration as *the messianic banquet*: they believed that the host at this feast at the end of time would be the Messiah. And now here is Jesus inviting 5,000 people to a meal.

Could this be a preview of the messianic banquet? If it is, that would make Jesus the Messiah.

Back in the story, the apostles are shocked at Jesus telling them to feed the crowd (see 13a). It can't be done, for they *have only five loaves of bread and two fish* (13).

Jesus has deliberately created a situation which is way too big for them.

The rest of the story is quickly told. Jesus gives God thanks for the bread and the fish, and gives them *to the disciples to distribute to the people* (16b).

Luke tells us that *they all ate and were satisfied* (17a). So each person hasn't just had a little food: they've had more than enough. And there are even leftovers: *the disciples picked up twelve basketfuls of broken pieces that were left over* (17b).

This is breathtaking. They have more food left at the end of the story than they had at the beginning.

This extraordinary miracle is indeed a preview of the messianic banquet (see John 6:14 for confirmation of this). So it tells us who Jesus is.

He is the Messiah.

3. – Peter's confession of Jesus (9:18-21)

We are in the middle of Block A. This is a conversation Jesus has been dreaming of.

He is in a secluded place with his disciples, and asks them *Who do the crowds say I am?* (18).

They mention some of the opinions on the street: John the Baptist, Elijah, one of the Old Testament prophets (see 19, see also chapter 9:7b-8).

So Jesus asks the question everything has been leading up to: *But what about you?* […] *Who do you say I am?* (20a).

Peter replies on behalf of them all: *God's Messiah* (20b).

And heaven stands still.

This is what the angel had told the shepherds (see chapter 2:11). Luke has already used the word *Messiah* in his Gospel (see 2:26, 3:15, 4:41), but this is the first time a human being has used the word of Jesus.

He is the Messiah, the saviour promised by God through the Old Testament prophets.

But Jesus *strictly warned them not to tell this to anyone* (21). Why this prohibition?

The reason is not hard to find. Popular expectation was that the Messiah would be a political king who would defeat the Romans so that Israel would be rid of the occupying power.

So the disciples are to tell no one that Jesus is the Messiah until they understand *what kind of Messiah* he is going to be.

He is about to answer that question for them.

4. – First prediction (9:22)

Jesus tells the disciples that *the Son of Man* (he's talking about himself) *must suffer many things and be rejected by the elders, the chief priests and the teachers of the law* (22a).

The leadership of Israel will turn against him, and this *must* happen.

But Jesus goes on: he *must be killed and on the third day be raised to life* (22b).

Why *must* these things happen? Jesus knows that this is the purpose of God the Father in sending him into the world: to suffer and to die.

And to rise again.

5. – Jesus: the call to discipleship (9:23-27)

Jesus talks now about what it costs to follow him: a person *must deny themselves and take up their cross daily* (23). Is this a hint about how he is going to die? He is certainly saying that all who follow a suffering Messiah must be willing to suffer themselves.

So Jesus spells out the results of deciding to live for ourselves: *Whoever wants to save their life will lose it* (24a). But for those who give their lives to serve Jesus and others there is good news: *Whoever loses their life for me will save it* (24b).

Jesus goes on to explain that there is no point in someone getting everything the world has to offer if they end up losing their very self (see 25).

And now he reaches the climax of what he wants to say: *If anyone is ashamed of me and my words, the Son of Man will be ashamed of them when he comes in his glory and in the glory of the Father and of the holy angels* (26). It's worth noticing that Jesus says, once again, that he is *the Son of Man.*

As we have seen, *Son of Man* is not always just Jesus' way of talking about himself: and here there is much more. He is saying that he is the glorious Son of Man depicted in the Old Testament prophecy of Daniel, to whom all the nations will belong.

Daniel had a vision of *one like a son of man coming with the clouds of heaven. He approached the Ancient of Days and was led into his presence* (see Dan 7:13).

This is not a coming *from* God, but a coming *to* God, which was fulfilled in the ascension and exaltation of Jesus after his resurrection.

The end of the paragraph might surprise us: *Truly I tell you,* says Jesus, *some who are standing here will not taste death before they see the kingdom of God* (27).

If Jesus is talking about his Second Coming in glory at the end of history, he was wrong. But, as we have just seen, the coming of the Son of Man described in Daniel 7:13 is a coming *to* God, not a coming *from* God.

So Jesus is referring here not to his Second Coming but to his resurrection and exaltation.

And of that, at the beginning of Block B, three of the disciples are about to get a preview.

B. Jesus is the Son (9:28-50)

1. – The transfiguration (9:28-36)

Jesus takes Peter, James and John up a mountain. As he was praying, *the appearance of his face changed, and his clothes became as bright as a flash of lightning* (29).

They are seeing the glorious Son of Man (see chapter 9:26).

Moses and Elijah join Jesus (see 30): perhaps they represent the Old Testament revelation in the Law and the Prophets. They are speaking *about his departure, which he was about to bring to fulfilment at Jerusalem* (31).

The word translated *departure* is literally *exodus* in Greek, and seems to look beyond the cross to the ascension of Jesus (see chapter 9:26 and 51).

Peter is in danger of seeing no real distinction between Moses, Elijah and Jesus: he suggests putting up shelters for all three (see 33). Luke tells us that Peter *did not know what he was saying* (33b).

But before he has finished his sentence they are enveloped in a cloud, and from it a voice says *This is my Son, whom I have chosen; listen to him* (35).

Luke adds that *when the voice had spoken, they found that Jesus was alone* (36a). The representatives of the Law and the Prophets give way to the one who fulfils both.

And that one is God's Son, declared authoritatively to be so by God the Father. And God adds this command to the disciples: *Listen to him* (35).

If Peter, James and John are able to think clearly after what they have experienced on the mountain, this extra sentence will have reminded them of Moses' words about the Prophet-Messiah who would come one day (see Deut 18:15). In Jesus these words are being fulfilled.

But Jesus is more than a prophet and more than the Messiah: he is the *Son of God*, in a unique relationship with the Father.

2. – Jesus drives out an evil spirit (9:37-43a)

A father asks Jesus to set his son free from a demon which tries to destroy him by throwing him *into convulsions so that he foams at the mouth* (39). He adds *I begged your disciples to drive it out, but they could not* (40).

Jesus seems to be disappointed by the nine disciples' lack of faith: he calls them an *unbelieving and perverse generation* (41a). When the boy is brought to him, *Jesus rebuked the demon, healed the boy and gave him back to his father* (42b).

No wonder *they were all amazed at the greatness of God* (43a).

3. – Second prediction (9:43b-45)

Jesus says something designed to catch the disciples' attention: he tells them to *listen carefully to what I am about to tell you* (44a).

He repeats to all twelve disciples what he has already told them: *The Son of Man is going to be delivered into the hands of men* (44b).

Luke tells us bluntly that *they did not understand what this meant* (45a).

More: *It was hidden from them, so that they did not grasp it, and they were afraid to ask him about it* (45b).

Three times in verse 45 Luke has told us of the disciples' failure to see what Jesus is saying. Maybe they are afraid to ask because they don't want to know.

4. – "I am the greatest" (9:46-48)

The next thing that happens after Jesus' teaching about his future suffering is that the disciples start arguing *as to which of them would be the greatest* (46).

They are doing this despite the fact that it's being revealed to them that the one they are following is the Son of God.

Jesus knows what they're thinking (see 47a) and has a little child *stand beside him* (47b). The disciples are probably wondering what Jesus is up to: in first-century Jewish culture children were seen as unimportant.

Now Jesus tells the disciples *Whoever welcomes this little child in my name welcomes me; and whoever welcomes me welcomes the one who sent me* (48a).

This is not just about being nice to children. Jesus is talking about giving priority to people (of whatever age) who we might be tempted to look down on.

Jesus sums up by explaining that *it is the one who is least among you all who is the greatest* (48b).

It's the disciple who is willing to be seen as insignificant, says Jesus, who is the greatest.

5. – "We're the only ones" (9:49-50)

It looks like the disciple John is expecting praise from Jesus: *We saw someone driving out demons in your name and we tried to stop him, because he is not one of us* (49).

It's like he thinks that only the Twelve should be doing this kind of thing. But instead of congratulation, John and the other disciples receive a lesson from Jesus: *Do not stop him* (50a).

He gives them the reason: *Whoever is not against you is for you* (50b). The exorcist the disciples had tried to stop driving out demons was doing it *in Jesus' name,* so he is clearly on the Jesus team too.

We have come to the end of Part One of Luke's Gospel. Jesus has chosen and is training twelve apostles, but the number of disciples is much greater than that.

I don't know about you, but seeing the Twelve begin to recognise that Jesus is the Messiah and the Son of God makes me want to go straight on into Part Two. But before looking forward, let's look back.

Learning the Gospel

I hope you see the value of learning Section Three: it's a great thing to have these events in our memories.

Begin by learning the two headings in bold. (And remember that doing this out loud will make it easier and quicker.)

Then learn the five incident titles for Block A: as you do so you will be surprised how many of the details you will find yourself remembering.

Then do the same with Block B.

You will find it a help to have arranged with a friend that both of you will do this.

It won't take you long to learn Section Three, as it's very short. If you run it through your mind once or twice a day, it will soon be in your long-term memory.

Section Three: Recognising Jesus

Introduction: Jesus sends out the twelve apostles

A. Jesus is the Messiah
1. Herod: his question
2. Jesus feeds the 5,000
3. Peter's confession of Jesus
4. First prediction
5. Jesus: the call to discipleship

B. Jesus is the Son
1. The transfiguration
2. Jesus drives out an evil spirit
3. Second prediction
4. "I am the greatest"
5. "We're the only ones"

Meeting the Lord

Please remember that Luke's Gospel is not only there so we can have information about Jesus: it is also there so we can meet him.

Begin telling yourself (or the friend you are doing this with) the incidents in Block A, including as many details as you can. Then do the same with Block B.

As you re-tell the Jesus story, take the opportunity to thank him. Praise him that he is the Messiah and the Son of God. You might want to pray for people you know who haven't yet recognised Jesus.

And, all the while, the Holy Spirit will be using his word in your life. As you re-tell Luke you will be rediscovering Jesus.

Luke's Gospel
Part Two: The Kingdom
Chapter 9:51 – 19:27

Part Two of the Gospel of Luke is often called
the Central Section or the Travel Narrative.
This is because of what Luke writes as it begins:
Jesus resolutely set out for Jerusalem (9:51b).

We could take that to mean that these chapters
are a straight-line journey from Galilee in the north
to Jerusalem in the south,
with everything in chronological order.

But that is not the case, as one example will make clear.
Already in chapter 10 Jesus visits Martha and Mary (see 10:38-42);
but they live in Bethany, which is just outside Jerusalem.

Part Two explains what it means to live in **the Kingdom of God**.

It looks like Luke has divided it into three sections.
Luke signals the beginning of a new section with two things:
First, a geographical marker, making clear that
Jesus is still on his way to Jerusalem.
(You can find these at 9:51, 13:22 and 17:11.)

And, second, an important question.
Close to the geographical marker,
someone asks Jesus a question, which Luke then uses
to set the theme for the section that follows.
(You can find these at 9:54, 13:23 and 17:20.)

We will use these themes for our section headings
in **Part Two: The Kingdom**

Section Four	9:51 – 13:21	The Opposition to the Kingdom
Section Five	13:22 – 17:19	The Citizens of the Kingdom
Section Six	17:20 – 19:27	The Arrival of the Kingdom

Section Four: The Opposition to the Kingdom
Luke 9:51 – 13:21

From the very start of Jesus' journey to Jerusalem, there is opposition: some Samaritans reject him. As the opposition continues, especially from the religious leaders of Israel, Jesus persists in proclaiming the good news, and helps the disciples to understand how to deal with the hostility of others and their own anxieties. In other words, he answers the question *What does it look like to live in the kingdom of God?*

Mary has chosen what is better,
and it will not be taken away from her.

Luke 10:42b

Enjoying the View

+ **Geographical marker:** *As the time approached for him to be taken up to heaven, Jesus resolutely set out for Jerusalem* (9:51).
+ **Important question:** *Lord, do you want us to call fire down from heaven to destroy them?* (9:54).

(For the significance of the *geographical marker* and the *important question*, see **Luke's Gospel: Part Two** on page 81.)

A. What to do when opposition comes (1) (9:51 – 10:37)

1. Samaritan opposition (9:51-56)
2. Jesus and potential disciples (9:57-62)
3. Jesus sends out seventy-two disciples (10:1-20)
4. Jesus and his Father (10:21-24)
5. The parable of the good Samaritan (10:25-37)

B. What to do when opposition comes (2) (10:38 – 11:36)

1. Jesus at Martha and Mary's (10:38-42)
2. Jesus teaches about prayer (11:1-13)
3. Jesus is accused of working with Satan (11:14-28)
4. Jesus teaches about judgment (11:29-32)
5. Jesus urges generosity (11:33-36)

C. God is Father as well as Judge (11:37 – 12:48)

1. Jesus condemns the Pharisees and the scribes (11:37-54)
2. Fear God and confess Jesus (12:1-12)
3. The parable of the rich fool (12:13-21)
4. Don't worry and trust God (12:22-34)
5. Disciples keep serving Jesus (12:35-48)

D. Make sure which side you're on (12:49 – 13:21)

1. Jesus promises division (12:49-53)
2. Jesus tells us to live wisely (12:54-59)
3. Jesus tells us to repent (13:1-9)
4. Jesus heals on the Sabbath (13:10-17)
5. Jesus promises growth (13:18-21)

In Part Two of the Gospel Luke continues to divide his material into blocks of five incidents: again, this is a help for the memory.

Blocks A and B provide us with ten lessons for disciples when opposition comes; Block C reminds us that disciples can trust God, whatever the circumstances; and Block D encourages us to commit to following Jesus and explains what that involves.

Please take a few minutes to read through Luke's account from chapter 9:51 to chapter 13:21. It's a long section, but it is worth taking the time to do this. As you do, take the opportunity to stop and to talk to Jesus.

Ask him questions and give him your heart.

Unpacking the Content

Luke tells us with his geographical marker that Jesus is starting out for Jerusalem (see chapter 9:51). Then, when he encounters opposition in Samaria, two of the disciples ask a question: *Lord, do you want us to call fire down from heaven to destroy them?* (see chapter 9:54).

The question sets the scene for Section Four: How should disciples react when they meet with opposition to Jesus and his kingdom?

A. What to do when opposition comes (1) (9:51 – 10:37)

Luke has arranged this material so that we can remember it.

Incidents 1 and 5 both involve Samaritans (negative, and then positive); and incidents 2 and 4 show us Jesus' relationship with potential disciples and with his Father.

And in the middle of the block we see that Jesus wants the kingdom of God to be proclaimed.

1. – Samaritan opposition (9:51-56)

Thus far Jesus has been in Galilee for most of his ministry. But now he *resolutely set out for Jerusalem* (51b). And his ultimate goal is not the crucifixion but the ascension: *the time approached for him to be taken up to heaven* (51a).

Most Jews would walk through Samaria on their way south, but there are people here who *did not welcome him, because he was heading for Jerusalem* (53).

So James and John have a helpful suggestion: *Lord, do you want us to call fire down from heaven to destroy them?* (54). They are living up to the nickname Jesus had given them: *sons of thunder* (see Mark 3:17).

But *Jesus turned and rebuked them* (55). In other words, the lesson for disciples who encounter opposition when proclaiming the good news, is simple: *Don't retaliate* (and see chapter 6:27-29).

2. – Jesus and potential disciples (9:51-56)

Now Luke introduces us to three possible candidates for being involved in the proclamation of the good news of the kingdom.

First, a man who claims too much (57-58). He is full of enthusiasm as he tells Jesus *I will follow you wherever you go* (57).

Jesus replies that *foxes have dens and birds have nests, but the Son of Man has nowhere to lay his head* (58). The fact that we read no more about this man suggests that he decides not to follow Jesus after all.

Second, a man who offers too little (59-60). Jesus starts out by telling this man *Follow me* (59a). But the man asks Jesus to *first let me go and bury my father* (59b).

Jesus' answer might sound harsh: he tells the man to *let the dead bury their own dead* (60a). But the father is almost certainly still alive: the funeral is a long way off. So Jesus is not telling the man he should not go to his father's funeral; rather he is telling him that putting off real discipleship until his father has died means that he is not willing for Jesus to take precedence over everything else.

Third, a man with wrong priorities (61-62). All this man wants is to *say goodbye to my family* (61).

But Jesus sees that this is not just someone loving his family, but a man who thinks family ties are in the end more important than following Jesus. So his reply is blunt: Jesus tells the man that *no one who puts a hand to the plough and looks back is fit for service in the kingdom of God* (62).

Just as a ploughman who looks back is likely to produce a crooked furrow, Jesus is saying that we can't be his disciples if we are hankering for other things: the job demands everything we are and everything we have.

Jesus said it to the second potential disciple, and he says it to us: *You go and proclaim the kingdom of God* (60b).

But the lesson from this incident is clear: *Give everything.*

3. – Jesus sends out the seventy-two disciples (10:1-20)

Jesus has already sent out the twelve apostles on a mission (see chapter 9:1-6); now he sends out a much larger group, presumably chosen from the many people who are following him (see chapter 6:13a and 17a).

Why seventy-two? Genesis chapter 10 lists seventy nations in the world (seventy-two in the Greek text), so perhaps the idea here is that one day the kingdom of God is going to be proclaimed to the whole world.

But not yet. Jesus is sending the seventy-two to Israel.

He is sending them *two by two ahead of him to every town and place where he was about to go* (1): they are to be like pairs of John the Baptists, preparing the way for Jesus and his message.

And the need is huge: *the harvest is plentiful, but the workers are few* (2a). Before these disciples leave they need to pray, asking *the Lord of the harvest* to *send out workers into his harvest field* (2b).

Doubtless Jesus wants *us* to pray that prayer too.

Now we learn more about what the seventy-two are going to do.

First, their mission (1-12). These disciples are to perform miracles and preach a message. Jesus says they will *heal those who are ill and tell them 'The kingdom of God has come near to you'* (9): it is the same task Jesus gave to the apostles (see chapter 9:2).

This will be tough, says Jesus: *I am sending you out like lambs among wolves* (3). In other words, there will be opposition. And even the customary greetings on the journey will take too much time away from the mission, so the disciples should *not greet anyone on the road* (4).

In first-century Jewish culture they could count on receiving hospitality, but they are not to *move around from house to house* (7b): they are not there for comfort but for proclamation.

But part of what the seventy-two do involves warning. If people reject their message they are to say *Even the dust of your town we wipe from our feet as a warning to you* (11a). But they will keep preaching the message that *the kingdom of God has come near* (11b).

Second, God's judgment (13-16). The seventy-two haven't left yet (see 16): they get to hear Jesus pronounce judgment on Capernaum (see 15) and on the two nearby towns of Chorazin and Bethsaida (see 13).

These towns, says Jesus, have witnessed enough miracles to inspire faith, and yet many people refused the message: *If the miracles that were performed in you had been performed in Tyre and Sidon, they would have repented long ago, sitting in sackcloth and ashes* (13b).

In other words Jesus is saying that some Galilean towns are more hardhearted than the pagan cities of Tyre and Sidon.

These words of judgment prepare us for Section Five of the Gospel, where the Jew/Gentile issue will at times take centre stage.

What Jesus is sending the seventy-two out to do is incredibly serious, because *whoever listens to you listens to me; whoever rejects you rejects me* (16a).

We don't know how long a time gap there is between verse 16 and verse 17: Luke tells us nothing about the disciples' experience of healing the sick and proclaiming the kingdom.

We get one piece of information, and that is from the seventy-two themselves.

Third, their return (17-20). They are full of joy after their first experience of being Jesus' messengers. They tell him *Lord, even the demons submit to us in your name* (17).

But Jesus doesn't want them to rejoice in the wrong things.

The devil's rebellion is something Jesus remembers: *I saw Satan fall like lightning from heaven* (18; see also Isa 14:12).

Yes, Jesus has given his disciples *authority* […] *to overcome all the power of the enemy* (19a). They can reckon with supernatural protection, for *nothing will harm you* (19b).

But that isn't what should be filling them with joy: *Do not rejoice that the spirits submit to you, but rejoice that your names are written in heaven* (20).

What delights us most should be knowing that we are accepted and loved by God (see also Phil 4:3).

There is something for every disciple to learn from this third incident in Block A: *Proclaim the kingdom.*

4. – Jesus and his Father (10:21-24)

This incident allows us to hear Jesus talking to his Father: *I praise you, Father, Lord of heaven and earth* (21a). No wonder he is *full of joy through the Holy Spirit* (21a).

As we listen to Jesus, it should bring us to worship. Luke shows us three things about him.

First, his joy (21). Jesus is glad that God doesn't reveal his truth to *the wise and learned,* but *to little children.* He doesn't mean literal little children – though of course it may include them – but people who might be seen as insignificant.

And God the Father has joy, too, says Jesus, in overturning human expectations in this way: *Yes, Father, for this is what you were pleased to do* (21).

Second, his status (22). Every phrase here should make our hearts beat faster. *All things have been committed to me by my Father,* says Jesus: not some things, but *all things.* And he adds that *no one knows who the Son is except the Father*: only God the Father knows Jesus completely and recognises that he is *the Son.*

This is talking about his divine status. Jesus is in unique relationship with God. We are on holy ground here.

The only person who knows God the Father perfectly and intimately is Jesus: *No one knows who the Father is except the Son* (22a). The sentence could have stopped there, but Jesus adds something which should make us catch our breath: no one knows who the Father is except the Son *and those to whom the Son chooses to reveal him* (22b).

We don't know God the Father completely of course; but if Jesus has opened our eyes we can say that we know God.

This should prompt us to honour Jesus: for who he is and for what he has done.

But there is something else about Jesus here.

Third, his encouragement (23-24). Luke tells us that Jesus now *turned to his disciples and said privately…* (23a): now he's probably talking just to the Twelve.

They are blessed to have had this revelation given to them, *for I tell you that many prophets and kings wanted to see what you see but did not see it, and to hear what you hear but did not hear it* (24).

Such people believed the promises about the coming of the Messiah, but they never got to experience the fulfilment and the reality.

And yet the disciples, in meeting Jesus, have been granted that privilege, because he is the Messiah and the Son of God (see chapter 9:20 and 35).

This is a massive encouragement to the disciples: they are *blessed* (23).

The lesson from this fourth incident in Block A is clear: *Honour the Son.*

5. – The parable of the good Samaritan (10:25-37)

At the beginning of the section we read about Samaritan opposition to Jesus; now, at the end, Jesus tells a story about a *good* Samaritan.

The hostility between Jews and Samaritans went back to the separation of Israel into the two kingdoms of Israel and Judah after the death of King Solomon. John writes in his Gospel that *Jews do not associate with Samaritans* (see John 4:9).

So it's impossible to overestimate the shock value of the story that Jesus is about to tell.

Before the parable, *an expert in the law stood up to test Jesus* (25a), which doesn't have to mean that he is trying to trap him: *What must I do to inherit eternal life?* (25b).

When Jesus asks him for a summary of the Old Testament Law, the scribe quotes two commandments: *'Love the Lord your God with all your heart and with all your soul and with all your strength and with all your mind',* and *'Love your neighbour as yourself'* (27, quoting Deut 6:5 and Lev 19:18).

Jesus agrees with his summary and adds *Do this and you will live* (28). This is not about earning acceptance from God: loving God like this implies a spiritual relationship that affects every aspect of life.

But the scribe is focusing on the second commandment and wants to know *Who is my neighbour?* (29).

So Jesus tells his story.

In the parable itself, a man is mugged and robbed on his journey between Jerusalem and Jericho. There are three attitudes to life exemplified in the story.

First, the attitude of the robbers: *What's yours is mine if I can get it* (30). *They stripped him of his clothes, beat him and went away, leaving him half-dead* (30b).

Second, the attitude of the priest and the Levite: *What's mine is mine if I can keep it* (31-32). Both men *passed by on the other side* (31b and 32b): their fear of becoming ritually unclean is greater than any concern they might have for their fellow-Jew.

Third, the attitude of the Samaritan: *What's mine is yours if you'll accept it* (33-35). The Samaritan has compassion on the wounded man (see

33b): *he went to him and bandaged his wounds, pouring on oil and wine* (34a).

Then, taking him to an inn, the Samaritan *took care of him* (34b) and gives money to the innkeeper, promising to *reimburse you for any extra expense you may have* (35b).

And he does all this, knowing that the man he is rescuing would in all likelihood despise him.

After the parable, Jesus asks the expert in the law *Which of these three do you think was a neighbour to the man who fell into the hands of robbers?* (36).

Perhaps the scribe doesn't want to say the words *The Samaritan*: instead he says *The one who had mercy on him* (37a).

And Jesus tells him to live like that (see 37b).

When we consider the historical context, Jesus is saying something extraordinary here. We are not to be choosy: we are to be neighbours to everyone, irrespective of who they are.

The lesson for disciples is plain for all to see: *Love your neighbour.*

In Block A the focus has been on what disciples should do when there is opposition to Jesus and the kingdom of God. And there have been five lessons for disciples, one from each of the five incidents: *Don't retaliate / Give everything / Proclaim the kingdom / Honour the Son /* and *Love your neighbour.*

Jesus was training his disciples *then*, and he is training us *now*.

But there are more lessons for us to learn in Block B.

B. What to do when opposition comes (2) (10:38 – 11:36)

1. – Jesus at Martha and Mary's (10:38-42)

Jesus, with his disciples, *came to a village where a woman named Martha opened her home to him* (38): only Martha is mentioned because she is the older of the two sisters.

Luke gives us a pen portrait of both of them.

First, Mary is listening (39). She sits *at the Lord's feet, listening to what he said.* And her body-language says it all: she's looking up at Jesus.

And she's listening.

Second, Martha is busy (40). Luke tells us that she is *distracted because of all the preparations that had to be made* (40a). Because she loves Jesus she has obviously decided to produce something special: and in any case preparing a meal for fifteen people (the disciples are there too) is a huge job.

It looks like the moment comes when Martha can stand it no longer.

She asks Jesus *Lord, don't you care that my sister has left me to do the work by myself?* And, assuming that he does care, she adds *Tell her to help me!* (40b).

Third, Jesus is clear (41-42). Jesus tells Martha that she is *worried and upset about many things* (41). But he goes on to say that *few things are needed – or indeed only one* (42a).

Jesus is being very clear: in the last analysis there is only one thing that matters, and that is listening to Jesus.

And Jesus underlines this by telling Martha: *Mary has chosen what is better, and it will not be taken away from her* (42b).

If we find ourselves thinking that Martha gets a raw deal here, that's because we underestimate the privilege of hearing what Jesus has to say.

Of course active service is important too, but the danger is sometimes that our service drowns out our listening.

We need to learn this lesson for the time when opposition comes: disciples must be people who *listen to Jesus.*

2. – Jesus teaches about prayer (11:1-13)

One of the disciples has a request: *Lord, teach us to pray, just as John taught his disciples* (1).

There are three parts to Jesus' answer.

First, a prayer (2-4). There is no indication here that Jesus is expecting his disciples to learn this by heart and recite it (though obviously there is no harm in that). Rather, the prayer reminds us of five things about God which should shape our praying.

He's our Father (2). Jesus himself addressed God in this way (see, for example, chapter 10:21), and he invites us to do the same. When we have come to know Jesus, we can call *his* Father *our* Father.

He's our King (2). Because God is Lord of the universe, we should pray that his name will be hallowed and honoured, and that more and more people will come into his kingdom.

He's our Carer (3). By asking God to *give us each day our daily bread* we are remembering that we are dependent on him to give us all we need.

He's our Forgiver (4a). Forgiveness is probably our greatest need (see chapter 5:20): the extraordinary thing is that God is willing to give us just that. And if we take this seriously we will be ready to *forgive everyone who sins against us* (4a).

He's our Protector (4b). Jesus is not implying that God tempts us (see James 1:13); rather he is encouraging us to ask our Father for spiritual protection from evil influences.

Second, a parable (5-10). Jesus asks us to imagine that we are wanting to borrow *three loaves of bread* from a friend at midnight, because an unexpected visitor has turned up (see 5-6).

Our friend replies *Don't bother me. The door is already locked, and my children and I are in bed. I can't get up and give you anything* (7).

But, says Jesus, you keep knocking and keep asking till your friend responds positively: *because of your shameless audacity he will surely get up and give you as much as you need* (8b).

The footnote in the NIV2011 suggests this alternative: our friend will get up and help us, *to preserve his good name* (8b footnote).

My guess is that this is what Jesus is getting at here. If our friend does nothing, his reputation in the village – his good name – will be damaged. In the same way, God answers our prayers not only because he loves us, but also *for the sake of his name* (see, for example, Psalm 23:3b, 25:11 and 31:3).

That should fill us with confidence as we pray. So, says Jesus, *Ask and it will be given to you; seek and you will find; knock and the door will be opened to you* (9).

And he underlines this, to encourage his disciples to pray: *Everyone who asks receives; the one who seeks finds; and to the one who knocks, the door will be opened* (10).

But Jesus has more to say.

Third, a picture (11-13). I suppose this is a parable too, but it isn't really a story. If a boy asks his father for a fish or an egg, his father is hardly going to give him a snake or a scorpion (see 11-12).

Even human fathers, *though you are evil* (13, compared to God), do good to their children, so disciples can be confident when they pray.

Jesus says it himself: *How much more will your Father in heaven give the Holy Spirit to those who ask him!* (13). The Spirit is the greatest gift of all, so if God is willing to give us his Spirit, he is willing to give us everything we need.

The lesson for disciples in incident 2 of Block B is clear: *Talk to God.*

3. – Jesus is accused of working with Satan (11:14-28)

Jesus sets a man free from a demon: it had robbed him of speech. Luke tells us that *when the demon left, the man who had been mute spoke, and the crowd was amazed* (14).

But not everyone is impressed.

Some people are saying *By Beelzebul, the prince of demons, he is driving out demons* (15).

So Jesus is being accused of working with Satan. In reply, he has two things to say to the crowd.

First, their thinking is muddled (17-22). If Jesus is working with the devil, then when he is driving out demons that means Satan is attacking Satan: that simply doesn't make sense (see 17-18).

And what about others who expel demons? Jesus asks *By whom do your followers drive them out?* (19).

So Jesus is accusing his accusers: their thinking is muddled. What is actually happening is something extraordinary: *If I drive out demons by the finger of God, then the kingdom of God has come upon you* (20).

Jesus explains what he's saying with a short parable.

A strong man protects his own house and his possessions (see 21). But *when someone stronger attacks and overpowers him, he [...] divides up his plunder* (22). Satan is the strong man, and men and women are his possessions.

But *someone stronger* is Jesus: when he drives out demons he is setting people free.

Second, their neutrality is impossible (23-26). When it comes to Jesus, neutrality is out of the question, says Jesus, for *whoever is not with me is against me, and whoever does not gather with me scatters* (23).

Now Jesus illustrates the point in a dramatic way.

If an evil spirit is driven out of someone, it might say it will *return to the house I left* (24b). *When it arrives,* says Jesus, *it finds the house swept clean and put in order* (25). Then it goes and finds *seven other spirits more wicked than itself, and they go in and live there* (26a).

Once again, the house represents a person. The demon may have gone, but if there is nothing to replace it (ie the person is being 'neutral'), then they are in danger. As Jesus says, *the final condition of that person is worse than the first* (26b).

When it comes to our attitude to Jesus, sitting on the fence is not an option. Neutrality is out of the question.

As the incident draws to a close, a woman in the crowd calls out to Jesus *Blessed is the mother who gave you birth and nursed you* (27). What she means is *I wish I'd had a son like you!*

Jesus' reply is blunt: *Blessed rather are those who hear the word of God and obey it* (28). These are important words: Jesus takes every opportunity to say them (see chapter 6:47 and chapter 8:21).

We've seen how Jesus reacts when people say he is working with Satan: he reasons with his accusers.

And for disciples the lesson is clear: *Expect opposition.*

4. – Jesus teaches about judgment (11:29-32)

Back in verse 16 of this chapter, some people had asked Jesus for a sign.

Now Jesus says that the only thing they're going to get is *the sign of Jonah* (29b). What he means is that just as *Jonah was a sign to the Ninevites, so also will the Son of Man be* (Jesus is talking about himself) *to this generation* (30).

Jesus is greater than any king: *something greater than Solomon is here* (31b); and he is greater than any prophet: *something greater than Jonah is here* (32b).

So the Queen of Sheba (see 1 Kings 10:1-13) will have something to say on Judgment Day: she *will rise at the judgment with the people of this generation and condemn them, for she came from the ends of the earth to listen to Solomon's wisdom* (31).

And the people of Nineveh (see Jonah 3:4-5) will say something on Judgment Day too: they *will stand up at the judgment with this generation and condemn it, for they repented at the preaching of Jonah* (32).

It's important to notice the examples Jesus uses: the Queen of Sheba and the people of Nineveh were *Gentiles*. This is a theme Jesus took up in his sermon in the synagogue in Nazareth (see chapter 4:24-27; also chapter 10:14); he will return to it in Section Five of the Gospel.

So people on Judgment Day will be judged according to how they have responded to the *wisdom* and *preaching* of Jesus.

It's easy to see the lesson for disciples as they encounter opposition: *Remember God's judgment.*

Block B has one more ingredient.

5. – Jesus urges generosity (11:33-36)

Your eye, says Jesus, *is the lamp of your body* (34a). The eye helps us to see where we're going, so this is about purposeful living.

When your eyes are healthy (34b) is a picture-language way of talking about being generous; *when they are unhealthy* (34c) is a way of talking about being mean. This is clear from the Old Testament proverb which says *He who has a good eye will be blessed, for he gives his bread to the poor* (Prov 22:9, literal translation).

Jesus is saying that being generous with what we have will do us good: *your whole body is full of light* (34b), while being stingy will have the opposite effect: *your body also is full of darkness* (34c).

This is enough to make us ask ourselves the question: *What am I living for – God or possessions?*

Jesus is urging his disciples to share what God has given them. The lesson is *Be generous.*

In Block B, as in Block A, the focus has been on what disciples should do when opposition comes. And there have, once again, been five lessons for disciples, one from each of the five incidents: *Listen to Jesus / Talk to God / Expect opposition / Remember God's judgment / Be generous.*

Jesus is still training disciples today.

C. God is Father as well as Judge (11:37 – 12:48)

Because the main theme of Section Four is opposition to the kingdom of God, Jesus talks often about God's judgment on human sin.

Now, in Block C, we are reminded that those who have decided to follow Jesus can know God as their Father (see chapter 11:2).

But the issue of judgment is still present.

1. – Jesus condemns the Pharisees and the scribes (11:37-54)

When Jesus accepts a Pharisee's invitation to eat with him his host is *surprised when he noticed that Jesus did not first wash before the meal* (38). Because Jesus is a religious teacher, the Pharisee expects more from Jesus than he would from others.

Jesus is on the attack immediately: *You Pharisees clean the outside of the cup and dish, but inside you are full of greed and wickedness* (39).

The Pharisee makes no reply: indeed, he says nothing during the whole incident. Maybe he is shocked by Jesus calling the Pharisees *foolish people* (40a).

Interestingly, Jesus adds *Be generous to the poor, and everything will be clean for you* (41). At the end of Block B he had been urging disciples to be generous (see chapter 11:33-36).

As if he has not caused enough offence, Jesus now launches into a condemnation of the religious elite, with three accusations aimed at the Pharisees and three aimed at the scribes. Each time he begins with the words *Woe to you...*

So here is Jesus denouncing the religious leadership of Israel. He starts with the Pharisees.

The first woe (42): You're missing the main thing! These leaders pay a lot of attention to obeying the tithing laws: *You give God a tenth of your mint, rue and all other kinds of garden herbs* (42a).

Jesus is not knocking that. But, he says, *You neglect justice and the love of God. You should have practised the latter without leaving the former undone* (42b).

The main thing is to love God and our neighbour (see chapter 10:27-28). But the Pharisees are missing this completely.

The second woe (43): You're full of pride! The Pharisees *love the most important seats in the synagogue* (43a): they are obviously more interested in being admired than in serving God and their fellow-Jews.

They also love *respectful greetings in the market-places* (43b). Wherever they are, they want to be the centre of attention.

The third woe (44): You're spiritually dead! The Pharisees are *like unmarked graves, which people walk over without knowing it* (44).

Their outward respectability conceals behaviour which is morally unclean and results in spiritual death.

One of the scribes says they are feeling insulted by what they're hearing (see 45); so now Jesus turns to them.

The fourth woe (46): You're weighing people down with impossible burdens! These *experts in the law* (46a) are insisting that everyone keeps laws and regulations which *they can hardly carry* (46b).

And, to make matters worse, they *will not lift one finger to help them* (46c).

Jesus is not holding back: he's angry.

The fifth woe (47-51): You're as guilty as your ancestors! By honouring the memory of their ancestors they approve of what they did: *they killed the prophets, and you build their tombs* (48).

Jesus adds that God, in his wisdom, said *I will send them prophets and apostles, some of whom they will kill and others they will persecute* (49).

Which is exactly what is happening.

So, says Jesus, *This generation will be held responsible for the blood of all the prophets that has been shed since the beginning of the world* (50). His language could not be any stronger.

When he adds *from the blood of Abel to the blood of Zechariah* (51a), Jesus is talking about the first and last martyrs of the Old Testament (see Gen 4:10 and 2 Chron 24:20-22 [2 Chronicles was the last book of the Jewish Bible]).

This is so important that Jesus repeats it: *Yes, I tell you, this generation will be held responsible for it all* (51b).

The sixth woe (52): You're preventing people from knowing God! The scribes, whose job was to teach the Law, *have taken away the key to knowledge* (52a).

Jesus continues: *You yourselves have not entered, and you have hindered those who were entering* (52b).

When people listen to teachers they should understand more, not less; it's like the the scribes are slamming the door of knowledge in people's faces.

We can only imagine how the Pharisees and the scribes are feeling because of their denunciation by Jesus. But Luke tells us what they do: they *began to oppose him fiercely and to besiege him with questions, waiting to catch him in something he might say* (53b-54).

It looks like this has been a turning-point. From now on the opposition from the religious leadership will only increase.

2. – Fear God and confess Jesus (12:1-12)

Despite the opposition, Jesus has a large following: *a crowd of many thousands had gathered, so that they were trampling on one another* (1a). But what Jesus says now is meant for those who are following him: *He began to speak first to his disciples* (1b).

So he has a warning for them: *Be on your guard against the yeast of the Pharisees, which is hypocrisy* (1c).

This will all be judged by God, for *there is nothing concealed that will not be disclosed, or hidden that will not be made known* (2; see also chapter 8:17).

We don't know how the disciples feel about Jesus being on collision course with the Pharisees and the scribes. But Jesus does.

And he tells them to do two things.

First, fear God (4-7). Jesus wants to comfort his disciples: *My friends, do not be afraid of those who kill the body and after that can do no more* (4).

Instead they should *fear him who, after your body has been killed, has authority to throw you into hell* (5). Fearing God doesn't mean being afraid of him; rather it means recognising him as the ultimate authority and judge.

Having that kind of relationship with God results in the assurance that he will look after us. *Are not five sparrows sold for two pennies?* asks Jesus; *Yet not one of them is forgotten by God. […] You are worth more than many sparrows* (6 and 7b).

So, rather than being afraid of what people can do to them, disciples are to fear God.

But there is something else.

Second, confess Jesus (8-12). Jesus says here that the verdict on Judgment Day depends on one's willingness on earth to be known as a disciple of Jesus: *Whoever publicly acknowledges me before others, the Son of Man will also acknowledge before the angels of God* (8).

And the opposite is true, too. If we disown Jesus or avoid admitting that we follow him, we *will be disowned before the angels of God* (9).

I guess every disciple of Jesus sometimes disowns him. But he has good news for us: *Everyone who speaks a word against the Son of Man will be forgiven* (10a). We can ask for forgiveness and start again.

But what does Jesus mean when he says that *anyone who blasphemes against the Holy Spirit will not be forgiven* (10b)?

The blasphemy against the Holy Spirit is the only sin that can never be forgiven, because it's a sin that no one repents of. It's not just saying that we don't believe; it's saying, *in the full knowledge that the good news of Jesus is true*, that it's a lie.

If we persist in that attitude the time will come when we have so hardened our hearts that we are no longer *able* to repent.

One more thing is worth adding here. Although Jesus warns in the Gospel accounts about the blasphemy against the Holy Spirit, he never tells anyone that thay have committed this sin.

So disciples are to confess Jesus, to be open about the fact that they follow him. And if that leads to arrest and trial, says Jesus, *do not worry about how you will defend yourselves or what you will say* (11b).

And he tells us why: it's because *the Holy Spirit will teach you at that time what you should say* (12).

The message is clear. When opposition comes, a disciple should fear God and not people, and confess Jesus openly, leaving the consequences to him.

Jesus is preparing his disciples for what is to come.

3. – The parable of the rich fool (12:13-21)

Now judgment takes centre stage again.

The story is prompted by a man asking Jesus to *tell my brother to divide the inheritance with me* (13). Jesus refuses to get involved, and then has a warning for everyone: *Be on your guard against all kinds of greed* (15a).

And he tells a parable to explain why that's important.

It's about a problem *a certain rich man* has (16): because the harvest has been so good this year, he realises that *I have no place to store my crops* (17b).

But he has the solution: he decides to *tear down my barns and build bigger ones* (18a). The man adds *And I'll say to myself, 'You have plenty of grain laid up for many years. Take life easy; eat, drink and be merry'* (19).

Maybe the crowd are on the man's side; perhaps they're impressed by his success and his planning.

But God sees things differently. Jesus tells us that *God said to him, 'You fool! This very night your life will be demanded from you. Then who will get what you have prepared for yourself?'* (20).

God sees what we do in secret (see chapter 12:2-3) and hears what we say to ourselves. There is going to be a Judgment Day, and we forget it at our peril.

Jesus ends by telling the crowd that the same thing will happen to *whoever stores up things for themselves but is not rich towards God* (21).

This is a story to make us think.

The danger with all of us is that we think the solution to our problems is bigger barns. But, as Jesus said in his introduction to the parable, *life does not consist in an abundance of possessions* (15b).

If I'm self-indulgent and living for me, I am not *rich towards God* (21b). Jesus' disciples should be generous, not greedy (15a, and see my comments on chapter 11:33-36).

4. – Don't worry and trust God (12:22-34)

This fourth part of Block C is a pair with the second. In both of them Jesus is teaching disciples that opposition to the message of the kingdom of God doesn't mean they're on their own.

God is with them. And *he cares.*

Once again, Jesus tells his disciples to do two things.

First, don't worry (22-26). Jesus is very blunt: *Do not worry about your life* (22). And he tells us why this makes sense.

Life is more than things like what we eat or wear (23). More: God looks after the ravens, and, says Jesus to his disciples, *How much more valuable you are than birds!* (24).

And there's another thing. Worrying doesn't actually achieve anything: *Who of you by worrying can add a single hour to your life?* (25).

So if we decide to stop worrying, what does Jesus want us to put in its place?

Second, trust God (27-34). After reminding the disciples how God looks after the grass and the flowers, Jesus adds *How much more will he clothe you – you of little faith!* (28b).

He's encouraging us to trust God.

Jesus reinforces this by reminding the disciples that *the pagan world runs after all such things* (30a), whereas *they* can be sure that *your Father knows that you need them* (30b).

Jesus explains what trusting God looks like: we are to *seek his kingdom* (31a). This is what should be preoccupying us: living for God's glory and longing for others to acknowledge his rule (see chapter 11:2).

And if we get our priorities right in this way we will experience God looking after our material needs: *Seek his kingdom, and these things will be given to you as well* (31b).

Jesus ends with encouragement to trust God and seek his kingdom: *Do not be afraid, little flock, for your Father has been pleased to give you the kingdom* (32, see also chapter 8:10a). This is not something they have earned: it is a gift from God their Father.

Our relationship with *stuff* says a lot about us. *Where your treasure is,* says Jesus, *there your heart will be also* (34). What I think about most tells me what I treasure most: is it material possessions or is it my heavenly Father and his glory?

Luke has one more ingredient for us in Block C.

5. – Disciples keep serving Jesus (12:35-48)

The theme of this paragraph is set by the first sentence. Jesus tells his disciples to *be ready for service and keep your lamps burning* (35).

This is a contrast to the religious leaders at the beginning of the block: the scribes load the people down with rules and regulations and then *will not lift a finger to help them* (see chapter 11:46b).

The parables here are about a master who has gone away to *a wedding banquet* (36) and will one day return: his servants are to continue to serve him until they see him again. The master represents Jesus, and the servants are all those who say that they follow him.

So the return of the master is presumably pointing to the return of Jesus in glory one day: he will teach about this in Section Six of the Gospel (see chapter 17:22-37).

Jesus tells two parables here. Peter's question in the middle of this incident helps us see that Jesus is addressing two groups.

First, everyone in the Jesus community (35-40). Jesus says that *it will be good for those servants whose master finds them watching when he comes* (37a).

If Jesus really is referring to his own return at the end of history, the next thing he says is extraordinary: the master *will dress himself to serve, will make them recline at the table and will come and wait on them* (37b).

Is Jesus saying that on the new earth he will serve his people?

But for now all the master's servants need to be watching and *ready* (38): disciples need to be actively serving Jesus. And we don't know when his return is going to be: talking about himself, Jesus says that *the Son of Man will come at an hour when you do not expect him* (40b).

So we all need to keep serving Jesus.

Peter now asks Jesus *Lord, are you telling this parable to us, or to everyone?* (41). So Jesus, in reply, has a parable for a specific group.

Second, leaders in the Jesus community (42-46). Now Jesus is talking about *the faithful and wise manager, whom the master puts in charge of his servants* (42). So this is not talking about all disciples, but about those who lead them.

Once again, the message is that the manager needs to be fully engaged in his master's absence with the task of giving the servants *their food allowance at the proper time* (42b-43).

But if the manager instead *begins to beat the other servants, both men and women, and to eat and drink and get drunk* (45), he will be punished. On his return, the master will *cut him to pieces and assign him a place with the unbelievers* (46b).

Jesus is saying that someone who is part of the Jesus community, or even a leader within it, may not really be in relationship with him at all.

This is a warning to all disciples. We don't become real members of the Jesus community by our service; rather we show by our service that we are real members of the Jesus community.

Jesus finishes by explaining a little more about the punishment of those who turn out to be *unbelievers* (46b). The one who *knows the master's will and does not get ready or does not do what the master wants will be beaten with many blows* (47).

But the one who does not know and does things deserving punishment will be beaten with few blows (48a): the punishment is different.

So those who are knowingly negligent will be punished more severely than those who have acted in ignorance.

The message is clear. As Jesus said at the start, disciples will be involved in actively serving their master Jesus: *Be dressed ready for service and keep your lamps burning* (35).

We have reached the end of Block C. God is certainly going to judge: Jesus teaches that in incidents 1, 3 and 5. But, sandwiched in between in incidents 2 and 4, are encouragements to disciples to fear God and to trust him.

Luke has one more block for us in Section Four: it's essential reading when we encounter opposition to Jesus and his kingdom.

D. Make sure which side you're on (12:49 – 13:21)

Jesus wants everyone to make sure if they're on his side or on the side of
the opposition. In Block D he helps us achieve certainty as to where we
stand.

1. – Jesus promises division (12:49-53)

Jesus begins by saying that he has *come to bring fire on earth* (49), and he
links this with the reality that *I have a baptism to undergo* (50). The baptism
is an image for the suffering Jesus will go through (see also Mark 10:38).

Now Jesus asks a question: *Do you think I came to bring peace on earth?*
(51a).

We might think that the answer is Yes: the angels had promised peace at his
birth (see chapter 2:14), and Jesus had sent out the seventy-two disciples to
proclaim peace (see chapter 10:5).

But Jesus answers his own question: *No, I tell you, but division* (51b).

The reason is simple. As the message of peace is proclaimed by Jesus and
his disciples, people will take opposite sides in relation to him (see chapter
2:34-35a).

Even families will experience this division, says Jesus. And he gives some
examples: *They will be divided, father against son and son against father...*
(53).

All the more reason for each of us to make sure where we stand.

2. – Jesus tells us to live wisely (12:54-59)

The crowds, says Jesus, are good at weather-forecasting because they look
at the available evidence, in clouds and in wind (see 54-55).

But why don't they show the same common sense when it comes to day-
to-day living? Jesus is puzzled, and asks *How is it that you don't know how
to interpret this present time?* (56b).

And because they don't show this basic wisdom he calls them *hypocrites*
(56a).

Jesus provides them with an example. If one of them is in disagreement with
someone else, he should *try hard to be reconciled* (58a), *or your adversary
may drag you off to the judge,* which might land you in prison (58b).

So it obviously makes sense to try for reconciliation. It's the common-
sense thing to do.

Disciples are going to want to live wisely. Jesus will have more to say about this in Block C of Section Five.

3. – Jesus tells us to repent (13:1-9)

This paragraph is not here to answer questions about undeserved suffering. Rather, it's here because Jesus wants us to see that repentance is essential for all those who follow him.

There are two examples here. The first is *the Galileans whose blood Pilate had mixed with their sacrifices* (1); the second is the *eighteen who died when the tower in Siloam fell on them* (4a).

Jesus is not interested in the details, but in the question: Do the crowds think these people were *worse sinners* (2) or *more guilty* (4b) than anyone else? It's clear what Jesus thinks the answer is.

So now comes the punchline – twice: *Unless you repent, you too will all perish* (3 and 5). All of us are guilty, so all of us need to repent.

Jesus goes on to tell a short parable. A man has a fig-tree: *he went to look for fruit on it but did not find any* (6). So he decides to cut it down: if there is no change after three years (see 7), what's the point of keeping it?

In the Old Testament the fig-tree is often used as a picture of Israel (see Hosea 9:10 and Micah 7:1). The fruit that Jesus is looking for in Israel, and in all his disciples, is repentance: a change of behaviour and an acceptance of God's rule in their lives.

But the man who looks after the vineyard suggests to the owner that he should give it one more year: *If it bears fruit next year, fine! If not, then cut it down* (9).

Jesus is saying two things here: God gives Israel, and all of us, time to repent; but the opportunity will not be there for ever.

If we are not willing to repent and live God's way, that suggests we're not on the Jesus team at all.

4. – Jesus heals on the Sabbath (13:10-17)

Only half of this paragraph describes the miracle: it's what happens after it that Luke directs our attention to.

Jesus is teaching in a synagogue on the Sabbath, and there's a woman there *who had been crippled by a spirit for eighteen years* (11a). She is in a very bad way: *She was bent over and could not straighten up at all* (11b).

So Jesus calls her forward and says *Woman, you are set free from your infirmity* (12b). And he puts his hands on her.

Luke tells us that *immediately she straightened up and praised God* (13).

Someone who *isn't* praising God is the synagogue leader, who is *indignant because Jesus had healed on the Sabbath* (14a). In other words, Jesus is not keeping the rules.

The synagogue leader tells the congregation *There are six days for work. So come and be healed on those days, not on the Sabbath* (14b). A woman has been released from eighteen years of suffering and the people are praising God: but the synagogue leader's complaining that Jesus has broken the Sabbath law.

But Jesus is not taking this lying down: the leader and others like him are *hypocrites* (15a). He gives them an example: *Doesn't each of you on the Sabbath untie your ox or donkey from the stall and lead it out to give it water?* (15b).

The answer is Yes. So Jesus asks *Then should not this woman, a daughter of Abraham, […] be set free on the Sabbath from what bound her?* (16).

The listeners' reaction proves the truth of what Jesus had said at the beginning of Block D: he brings division. Luke tells us that *all his opponents were humiliated, but the people were delighted with all the wonderful things he was doing* (17).

This incident provides us with another way of discovering if we really belong to Jesus. Do I want to live for God's glory and God's kingdom, or am I focused on religious rules?

The whole of Section Four in Luke's Gospel has been about opposition to the kingdom message of Jesus. But it ends with a reassurance for all his disciples.

5. – Jesus promises growth (13:18-21)

At the beginning of Block D Jesus promised division. Now, at its end, he promises growth: the kingdom of God will grow.

To make the point, he tells two parables.

First, the mustard seed (18-19). There was a proverb about a mustard seed being incredibly small, but *it grew and became a tree* (19a).

That, says Jesus, is what *the kingdom of God* is like (18). It starts with one man and his message, but it will grow into something huge.

There may be a hint of that in Jesus' comment that the mustard tree is so big, that *the birds perched in its branches* (19b). The Old Testament sometimes uses a tree as an image for a great empire (eg Dan 4:10-12), with the birds in its branches being the nations under the empire's protection (see Dan 4:20-22).

Is Jesus talking about the Gentiles coming into the kingdom of God? Will this be one reason why it will see the growth Jesus is promising here?

In any case the lesson from the mustard seed is clear: unspectacular beginnings lead to a triumphant climax.

But now Jesus tells a second parable.

Second, the yeast (20-21). A woman mixes some yeast *into about thirty kilograms of flour until it worked all through the dough* (21): this would make a meal for a hundred people.

This is another example for *the kingdom of God* (20): there will be extraordinary growth.

Disciples, who might be unnerved by the opposition to Jesus, need to hear this message.

And Jesus wants them to join his team. The three middle ingredients of Block D tell us three characteristics of Jesus disciples: they want to live wisely; they commit to repentance; and they are not bound by religious rules.

Yes, there will be division (see incident 1). But there will be astonishing growth too (see incident 5).

Learning the Gospel

First, learn the four block titles in bold: say them out loud several times and you will soon have remembered them.

Now go back to Block A. Say the five incidents until you can do it with your eyes closed. Then go on to Block B and do the same.

When you reach Block C, remember that incidents 1, 3 and 5 have God as Judge, while incidents 2 and 4 reassure disciples that he is their Father.

Then do the same for Block D.

And remember that this will be easier if you agree with a friend that both of you will do this, before meeting up to test each other.

As with every section, if you run the order of the incidents in Section Four through your mind a few times every day, it will soon be in your long-term memory.

Section Four
The Opposition to the Kingdom

A. What to do when opposition comes (1)
1. Samaritan opposition
2. Jesus and potential disciples
3. Jesus sends out the seventy-two disciples
4. Jesus and his Father
5. The parable of the good Samaritan

B. What to do when opposition comes (2)
1. Jesus at Martha and Mary's
2. Jesus teaches about prayer
3. Jesus is accused of working with Satan
4. Jesus teaches about judgment
5. Jesus urges generosity

C. God is Father as well as Judge
1. Jesus condemns the Pharisees and the scribes
2. Fear God and confess Jesus
3. The parable of the rich fool
4. Don't worry and trust God
5. Disciples keep serving Jesus

D. Make sure which side you're on
1. Jesus promises division
2. Jesus tells us to live wisely
3. Jesus tells us to repent
4. Jesus heals on the Sabbath
5. Jesus promises growth

Meeting the Lord

Begin to tell yourself the ingredients of Block A: you will be surprised how many details come back to you, and you can take a look at your Bible if your mind goes blank!

In Block A it will help you to remember the lessons taught here: *Don't retaliate / Give everything / Proclaim the kingdom / Honour the Son /* and *Love your neighbour.*

Similarly, as you let the incidents of Block B run through your mind, remember the lessons: *Listen to Jesus / Talk to God / Expect opposition / Remember God's judgment /* and *Be generous.*

If you talk to God as you do all this, that will turn an intellectual exercise into a spiritual encounter.

When you are telling yourself (or your friend) Block C, remember that God is Father as well as Judge. And the middle three incidents of Block D, which starts and finishes with a promise, help us to know if we really belong to Jesus: *Do I want to live according to God's wisdom? / Do I want to live in daily repentance? / Do I want to live for God's kingdom, or am I just interested in keeping rules?*

It is so worthwhile to take time to go through Section Four in your mind: as you re-tell Luke you will be rediscovering Jesus.

Section Five: The Citizens of the Kingdom
Luke 13:22 – 17:19

Jesus is still on his journey from Galilee to Jerusalem. In Section Four he was equipping his disciples to face opposition, and continuing to proclaim the good news of the kingdom of God. Now, in Section Five, in answer to a question, Jesus explains the characteristics of those who belong to him: What kind of people are the disciples of Jesus?

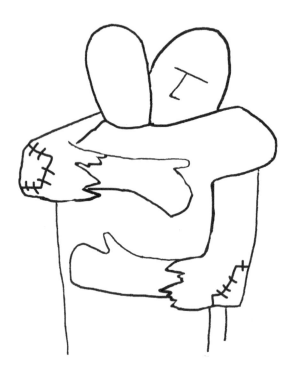

He ran to his son,
threw his arms round him
and kissed him.

Luke 15:20b

Enjoying the View

+ **Geographical marker:** *Then Jesus went through the towns and the villages, teaching as he made his way to Jerusalem (13:22).*
+ **Important question:** *Lord, are only a few people going to be saved? (13:23).*

(For the significance of the *geographical marker* and the *important question*, see **Luke's Gospel: Part Two** on page 81.)

A. Jews and Gentiles who count the cost (13:22 – 14:35)

1. The narrow door and the messianic banquet (13:22-30)
2. Jesus' sorrow over Jerusalem (13:31-35)
3. Jesus at a Pharisee's house (14:1-14)
4. The parable of the great banquet (14:15-24)
5. The cost of discipleship (14:25-35)

B. ...who know they were lost (15:1-32)

1. The Pharisees and the scribes (15:1-2)
2. The parable of the lost sheep (15:3-7)
3. The parable of the lost coin (15:8-10)
4. The parable of the lost son (15:11-24)
5. What happened to the older brother (15:25-32)

C. ...and who want to live wisely (16:1 – 17:19)

1. The parable of the wise manager (16:1-9)
2. Jesus teaches about God's wisdom (16:10-18)
3. The parable of the rich man and Lazarus (16:19-31)
4. Wisdom in the Jesus community (17:1-10)
5. Jesus heals ten lepers (17:11-19)

Luke has done what he always does: he has divided the section into blocks of five incidents each.

In Block A we encounter a fuller treatment of a topic that we have already come across in the Gospel: Is the kingdom of God only for Jews, or are Gentiles invited too?

In Block B Jesus explains that disciples are people who know that they were lost and needed to be found by a God who seeks them.

And in Block C we learn that the citizens of the kingdom commit to living according to God's revealed wisdom.

Before reading any further in *The Luke Experiment*, please read chapter 13:22 to chapter 17:19 in Luke's Gospel. As you do, talk to God about what you are hearing from Jesus, and ask him to make you more and more the kind of disciple Jesus is looking for.

I am praying that, as you read these chapters, you will meet Jesus.

Unpacking the Content

Luke reminds us with his geographical marker that Jesus is still on his way to Jerusalem (see chapter 13:22). Then someone asks him *Lord, are only a few people going to be saved?* (verse 23).

The question sets the scene for Section Five: Who are Jesus' disciples?

A. Jews and Gentiles who count the cost (13:22 – 14:35)

1. – The narrow door and the messianic banquet (13:22-30)

This is about entering the kingdom of God or, in terms of the question which begins Section Five, who will be saved. Jesus says that many people *will try to enter and will not be able to* (24b).

This is why Jesus tells us to *make every effort to enter through the narrow door* (24a). No one *drifts* into the kingdom of God.

There is something else one can say about the door, apart from the fact that it's narrow: it won't be open for ever. Jesus warns his listeners *Once the owner of the house gets up and closes the door, you will stand outside knocking and pleading* (25).

Who does the owner represent? Jesus doesn't tell us, but those who have been locked out of the kingdom shout to him through the door that *You taught in our streets* (26).

So the owner is Jesus; he is the King of the kingdom of God.

And twice he tells those who are shut outside *I don't know you* (25b and 27). In other words, salvation is not a matter of behaviour but of relationship: if we don't know Jesus he classes us as *evildoers* (27) and we don't belong in the kingdom.

Jesus makes this clear by talking about *the feast in the kingdom of God* (29b). He's referring to the messianic banquet, which is a poetic way of talking about what we might call heaven: it's a celebration hosted by the

Messiah himself (see my comments on the feeding of the 5,000 in chapter 9:10-17).

Jesus says there will be *weeping there, and gnashing of teeth, when you see Abraham, Isaac and Jacob and all the prophets in the kingdom of God, but you yourselves are thrown out* (28).

And, while many Jews will be missing, there will be many Gentiles there: *People will come from east and west and north and south and take their places at the feast in the kingdom of God* (29).

This is strong stuff. Many of Jesus' listeners would have said that the messianic banquet was exclusively for Jews, and now here he is, saying that many Jews will be excluded, to be replaced by believing Gentiles.

Jesus is turning expectations upside down. He adds that *there are those who are last who will be first, and first who will be last* (30).

2. – Jesus' sorrow over Jerusalem (13:31-35)

This incident follows on naturally from the previous one.

Told by a Pharisee that Herod wants to kill him, Jesus says to tell him *I will keep on driving out demons and healing people today and tomorrow, and on the third day I will reach my goal* (32). Nothing is going to deflect Jesus from doing what he has come to do.

And his goal is the capital, *for surely no prophet can die outside Jerusalem!* (33b).

And the very mention of Jerusalem fills Jesus with sorrow: *Jerusalem, Jerusalem, you who kill the prophets and stone those sent to you, how often I have longed to gather your children together, as a hen gathers her chicks under her wings* (34).

The image is tender: Jesus loves the people of Israel.

But he adds *You were not willing* (34b).

So judgment is coming: *Look, your house is left to you desolate* (35a). Jesus is almost certainly referring to the destruction of the temple by the Romans in AD70. The temple is a symbol of God's relationship with his people: when the people don't want the relationship, the temple is abandoned.

In order to repent, Israel would need to say, as a nation, what the crowds will shout when Jesus enters the city on a donkey: *Blessed is he who comes in the name of the Lord* (35b, see also chapter 19:38a and Ps 118:26).

But this is not a promise that they will.

In incident 3 Jesus' sorrow over his own people will only increase.

3. – Jesus at a Pharisee's house (14:1-14)

Luke tells us that Jesus is *being carefully watched* (1). *A prominent Pharisee* (1), who has invited Jesus for a meal, says nothing in this passage: Jesus is on the attack throughout.

It's like he's saying that there are three things which can keep people out of the kingdom of God.

First, keeping rules (2-6). *There in front of him was a man suffering from abnormal swelling of his body* (2): it looks like this is a set-up.

Jesus asks the Pharisees and the scribes who are there *Is it lawful to heal on the Sabbath or not?* (3); they have no reply.

Luke tells us that Jesus *healed him and sent him on his way* (4b).

So Jesus asks another question: *If one of you has a child or an ox that falls into a well on the Sabbath day, will you not immediately pull it out?* (5, and see chapter 13:15). It seems clear enough: there is something more important than Sabbath rules.

And they had nothing to say (6). Once again, the religious elite have no answer.

If we think religion is a matter of keeping rules, that will keep us out of the kingdom.

Second, looking good (7-11). Jesus describes a dinner party, because he notices how *the guests picked the places of honour at the table* (7).

If I'm invited to a feast and *take the place of honour* (8), I may have to give up my seat if *a person more distinguished* (8) has been invited too. It makes much more sense to *take the lowest place* (10): then the host might say *Friend, move up to a better place* (10).

This is not just a lesson about dinner-party etiquette.

If life for me is about looking good so as to be admired by others, I am not seeing things God's way. Jesus says that *all those who exalt themselves will be humbled, and those who humble themselves will be exalted* (11).

It's a world upside down. If my ambition is to look good, I am excluding myself from God's kingdom.

But there's a third thing that will make it impossible for us to be at the messianic banquet.

Third, being picky (12-14). Jesus is addressing his host directly (see 12a): he is embarrassing him in front of his guests.

He says *When you give a luncheon or dinner, do not invite your friends, your brothers or sisters, your relatives or your rich neighbours* (12a). The reason is simple: *If you do, they may invite you back and so you will be repaid* (12b).

Jesus is not saying we should never invite such people: he is using a Jewish way of speaking to communicate that we are not to be picky about who we invite. We are not just to invite *people like us.*

Rather, says Jesus, *invite the poor, the crippled, the lame, the blind, and you will be blessed* (13-14a). And the reward comes later: *You will be repaid at the resurrection of the righteous* (14b).

Jesus has mentioned three things which will keep us out of God's kingdom: keeping rules, looking good and being picky.

And he has said this to *a prominent Pharisee* (1).

But the dinner party is not over yet.

4. – The parable of the great banquet (14:15-24)

Perhaps because Jesus has just mentioned *the resurrection of the righteous* (14b), one of the guests says *Blessed is the one who will eat at the feast in the kingdom of God* (15). He's thinking of the messianic banquet.

So incident 4 really belongs here in Block A.

Jesus' response is to tell a parable. As we listen to it, there are three lessons he wants us to learn.

First, recognise the servant (16-17). A man is *preparing a great banquet and invited many guests* (16). When it's time for the feast *he sent his servant to tell those who had been invited, 'Come, for everything is now ready'* (17).

In Matthew's Gospel Jesus tells a similar story, but there the servants are in the plural (see Matt 22:1-14). But here the man has only one servant.

In the Old Testament prophecy of Isaiah, God introduces his servant in the so-called servant songs. In the first he begins *Here is my servant, whom I uphold, my chosen one in whom I delight* (Isa 42:1a). And in the last, God reveals that this will be a suffering servant who dies for the sins of others (see Isa 52:13 – 53:12).

The extraordinary thing is that, at the last supper before he goes to the cross, Jesus will quote from this last song and declare that *this must be fulfilled in me* (see Luke 22:37).

In other words, Jesus is the servant of the Lord who will take sinners' punishment onto his shoulders.

So Jesus is God's servant in the parable.

Second, don't make excuses (18-20). The invited guests give reasons why they can't come to the banquet: one has bought a field, one has bought some oxen and another has got married.

In the context of Block A it makes sense to see the invited guests as people from Israel: they don't want to listen to the servant, so they make excuses.

Jesus is encouraging his listeners not to make that mistake, but to make a positive decision. Which is what we turn to now.

Third, accept God's invitation (21-24). The owner becomes angry when he learns that the invited guests are now not coming to his banquet. So he says to his servant *Go out quickly into the streets and alleys of the town and bring in the poor, the crippled, the blind and the lame* (21b, and compare verse 13).

Even after the servant has done this there are still empty seats, so the master tells the servant to *go out to the roads and country lanes and compel them to come in, so that my house will be full* (23).

With the context of Block A to help us, it's clear that these other guests are Gentiles: they were not originally invited, but now they are being welcomed with open arms.

The master in the parable is very blunt: *Not one of those who were invited will get a taste of my banquet* (24).

The message is clear: God longs for us to accept his invitation.

5. – The cost of discipleship (14:25-35)

Luke tells us that *large crowds were travelling with Jesus* (1): perhaps many of them are considering committing themselves to becoming his disciples.

So Jesus tells them that they must do two things.

First, deny yourself (26-27). Jesus says *a person cannot be my disciple* (26b) unless they *hate father and mother, wife and children, brothers and sisters* (26a).

Jesus doesn't mean this literally. He's using a Jewish way of speaking to say that their love for family must pale into insignificance beside their love for him.

So of course we should love our families. But if we love our families more than we love Jesus, we have disqualified ourselves as potential disciples.

Jesus even says a disciple must *hate their own life* (26b): Jesus must be more important to me than I am to myself.

He spells this out by saying that *whoever does not carry their cross and follow me cannot be my disciple* (27). Jesus has said this before (see chapter 9:23), but clearly it needs to be said again.

Is this a hint about how he is going to die?

Crucifixion was a sufficiently common event in Roman-occupied Israel for people to understand immediately what Jesus meant. A disciple needs to put following Jesus above everything else, and must even be ready to die for him.

Second, count the cost (28-33). A builder who can't finish his building because the money runs out, hasn't counted the cost; and the same is true of a king who leads his troops into battle without first comparing the size of the two armies (see 28-32).

They deserve to be laughed at.

So, says Jesus, *those of you who do not give up everything you have cannot be my disciples* (33). Jesus must come first.

So all of us need to count the cost.

Receiving the kingdom is a gift of God's grace, but it will cost us everything we have.

Jesus ends with another pithy saying. If salt *loses its saltiness* (34), it might as well be thrown away. In the same way there is no point in being a Jesus disciple if I haven't denied myself and counted the cost.

This last incident of Block A invites us to draw a conclusion. From its context in the whole block we can see that Jews and Gentiles are equally welcome to start following Jesus and so enter the kingdom of God.

But everyone needs to know that discipleship has a cost.

Now, Block B will tell us more about the people who belong to Jesus.

B. ...who know they were lost (15:1-32)

There are, famously, three parables in this chapter of the Gospel: all three are about something lost being found. But the parable of the lost son has a sting in the tail, as Jesus talks about the reaction of the older brother. Luke includes this part for two reasons.

First, Jesus told the story this way; and second, it links back to the introduction to the whole chapter.

Which, intriguingly, creates a block of five incidents.

1. – The Pharisees and the scribes (15:1-2)

The Pharisees and the scribes have appeared together often in the Gospel (see, for example, chapter 5:21, 30; 6:11), and Jesus has launched at least one verbal attack on them (see chapter 11:37-53).

Now here they are again.

They see that *the tax collectors and sinners were all gathering round to hear Jesus* (1), and they don't like it. Luke tells us that they *muttered* (2).

Their complaint about Jesus is that *this man welcomes sinners, and eats with them* (2).

A respectable religious teacher should not be mixing with disreputable people, and sharing a meal with them is most decidedly a step too far.

Now, says Luke, *Jesus told them this parable* (3): what follows (and the same is true of the other two parables) is not primarily for the crowds but for the Pharisees and the scribes.

2. – The parable of the lost sheep (15:3-7)

If a shepherd has a hundred sheep and loses one, *doesn't he leave the ninety-nine in the open country and go after the lost sheep until he finds it?* (4b).

When he does find it, he goes home and throws a party for his friends and neighbours. He tells them to *rejoice with me; I have found my lost sheep* (6b).

Jesus doesn't just tell the story. He explains it too: *I tell you that in the same way there will be more rejoicing in heaven over one sinner who repents than over ninety-nine righteous people who do not need to repent* (7).

It looks like heaven explodes with joy when one sinner repents. When one person admits they need to change and commits to it, God rejoices.

But, says Jesus, there are people who think they're righteous and so don't think repentance could possibly be for them.

Are the Pharisees and the scribes listening? Are *we* listening?

3. – The parable of the lost coin (15:8-10)

So Jesus tells a second parable.

When a woman loses one of her ten silver coins, *doesn't she light a lamp, sweep the house and search carefully until she finds it?* (8b).

Because we've read the first parable we know what's coming. When she finds her coin she tells her friends and neighbours to *rejoice with me; I have found my lost coin* (9).

And, once again, Jesus explains: *In the same way, I tell you, there is rejoicing in the presence of the angels of God over one sinner who repents* (10).

Jesus could stop there: he has made his point. But a third parable is going to contain ingredients missing so far.

And have a sting in the tail, too.

4. – The parable of the lost son (15:11-24)

We'll look at the two main characters in the story: a father, and the younger of his two sons.

First, the younger son (12-20a). He says to his father *Father, give me my share of the estate* (12): he might just as well have said *I wish you were dead.*

Amazingly, his father gives him what he wants: it would be one third of the estate (see Deut 21:17). So the younger son leaves home, travels a long distance and *squandered his wealth in wild living* (13).

After some time there is *a severe famine in that whole country* (14b): this is after the younger son *had spent everything* (14a). So of course *he began to be in need* (14c). He goes and offers to work for a farmer, *who sent him to his fields to feed pigs* (15). Polite Middle-Easterners got rid of someone by offering them a job they couldn't possibly accept, and that is what the farmer is doing here.

A job feeding pigs is ultimate degradation for the younger son, but he feels like he has no choice. He is at rock bottom.

And alone: *No one gave him anything* (16b).

But then, says Jesus, *he came to his senses* (17a). He is *starving to death*, but his *father's hired servants have food to spare* (17b). So he decides to go home and say *Father, I have sinned against heaven and against you* (18).

He's not asking to be treated as one of the family again: he knows he doesn't deserve that. He's going to tell his father *I am no longer worthy to be called your son; make me like one of your hired servants* (19).

The word *repentance* isn't there in verses 17-19, but that's what Jesus is describing.

So the younger son starts on the journey home. But there's a surprise in store for him.

Second, the waiting father (20b-24). The father sees his son *while he was still a long way off* (20): he has obviously been watching and waiting, longing for this day. And he *feels* something: he is *filled with compassion for him* (20).

Now he does something that no self-respecting father would do: *he ran to his son* (20b). He is risking social humiliation. But it looks like he doesn't care: he *threw his arms round him and kissed him* (20), which is like a public declaration that the son is restored to his family.

The son begins his prepared speech, but the father doesn't let him finish. He's already talking to his servants, telling them to *bring the best robe,* to *put a ring on his finger and sandals on his feet* (22).

The father could not be more welcoming. But there's more.

There's going to be a party. Killing *the fattened calf* means that this is not just going to be for the close family: the whole village is going to be invited to the celebration.

The father's enthusiasm is there for all to see and hear: *This son of mine was dead and is alive again; he was lost and is found* (24).

It is no wonder that this story is so famous: the love of the father for his son is astonishing. As is God's love for us.

But there is more to come.

5. – What happened to the older brother (15:25-32)

As the older brother is coming towards the house, *he heard music and dancing* (25). When he asks one of the servants what's going on, he learns the news: *Your brother has come, [...] and your father has killed the fattened calf because he has him back safe and sound* (27).

It seems like it's good news for everyone else, but bad news for the older brother: he *became angry and refused to go in* (28a).

His father gets wind of this, so *went out and pleaded with him* (28b). But the older brother is having none of it: *All these years I've been slaving for you and never disobeyed your orders* (29a). He's always been a good son.

The younger son, he says, *has squandered your property with prostitutes* (30a). But he doesn't call him *my brother,* but *this son of yours*: he's almost refusing to acknowledge that the two of them are from the same family.

The older son is angry because, as he tells his father *You never gave me even a young goat so I could celebrate with my friends* (29b). But when the younger brother comes home, *you kill the fattened calf for him!* (30b).

Here's the problem: the older brother's father is *welcoming* the younger brother home, and putting on *a fantastic meal* for him.

This should remind us of what the Pharisees and scribes were muttering about at the beginning of the chapter: Jesus *welcomes sinners and eats with them* (2).

It's exactly the same complaint.

Just as the older brother thinks his father shouldn't welcome the younger son and eat with him, so the Pharisees and scribes think Jesus shouldn't welcome sinners and eat with them.

At the end of the parable the father tells his son that *everything I have is yours* (31b). But, he adds, *we had to celebrate and be glad, because this brother of yours was dead and is alive again; he was lost and is found* (32).

Jesus deliberately doesn't tell us how the older brother reacts: there is no verse 33 in Luke chapter 15. Have the Pharisees and the scribes got the point? Have they understood how they *should* be reacting to Jesus and his proclamation of the kingdom of God?

Luke's Block B in Section Five of his Gospel tells us more about the people who are part of the kingdom: they know they were lost.

And they know who has found them, too.

C. ...and who want to live wisely (16:1 – 17:19)

When people have been brought into God's kingdom, they want to live in ways that are wise; Jesus has already talked about this in Section Four (see *Jesus tells us to live wisely,* chapter 12:54-59).

1. – The parable of the wise manager (16:1-9)

There is a rich man, says Jesus, *whose manager was accused of wasting his possessions* (1). So the manager, whose dishonesty has been discovered, gets told *You cannot be manager any longer* (2b).

So he asks himself *What shall I do now?* (3a).

After rejecting the alternatives, he comes up with a plan: *I know what I'll do so that, when I lose my job here, people will welcome me into their houses* (4).

So he calls in *each of his master's debtors* (5a), and reduces the amount they owe (see 5-7): while working his notice he still has the authority to do this.

By doing this, the manager is making friends for himself.

Jesus now says that *the master commended the dishonest manager*, not for his dishonesty, but *because he had acted shrewdly* (8a; the word can also be translated *wisely*).

The danger is that *the people of this world are more shrewd in dealing with their own kind than are the people of the light* (8b), who should *use worldly wealth to make friends for yourselves* (9a).

We need to be clear: Jesus is not commending dishonesty.

But with his parable he is saying that it's a wise thing to use our resources to help others find their way into the kingdom of God. That explains why Jesus adds that living wisely in this way will result, one day, in our being *welcomed into eternal dwellings* (9b).

2. – Jesus teaches about God's wisdom (16:10-18)

Jesus follows up the parable by telling his disciples (see verse 1a) three things about wisdom: they will help us to live wisely.

First, wisdom teaches honesty (10-12). Jesus teaches basic common sense here: *Whoever can be trusted with very little can also be trusted with much, and whoever is dishonest with very little will also be dishonest with much* (10).

Not many people will argue with that.

So this means that what I'm like in *handling worldly wealth* (11) will lead to people either trusting me, or not trusting me, with theirs.

So honesty is the best policy.

Second, wisdom demands a choice (13-15). This, says Jesus, is because *no one can serve two masters* (13a). Someone, or something, has to have priority in our lives. So a decision needs to be made, because we *cannot serve both God and Money* (13c).

The wise thing to do is to decide to serve God.

It looks like the Pharisees have already made their choice: Luke tells us that they *loved money, heard all this and were sneering at Jesus* (14).

So he tells them *God knows your hearts* (15): they cannot hide from him. And Jesus finishes: *What people value highly is detestable in God's sight* (15b).

Once again, in his dealings with the Pharisees, he goes straight for the jugular.

Third, wisdom comes from God's word (16-18). Jesus wants to stress to his disciples, and to the religious leaders too, that he submits to the Scriptures: *The Law and the Prophets were proclaimed until John* (16a): he is talking about the whole of what we call the Old Testament.

Since then, *the good news of the kingdom of God is being preached* (16b, and see chapter 4:43).

But that doesn't mean that the Jewish Scriptures are now redundant. Jesus says *It is easier for heaven and earth to disappear than for the least stroke of a pen to drop out of the Law* (17).

And he provides an example: marriage and divorce. In first-century Jewish culture divorce carried with it the automatic right for both the man and the woman to remarry.

But Jesus says No: the person who does that *commits adultery* (18).

Back in the introduction to his Gospel Luke told us that the boy Jesus *was filled with wisdom* and *grew in wisdom* (chapter 2:40 and 52). Incident 2 is showing us the truth of that.

Wisdom comes from God's word. And people in the kingdom of God want to act wisely.

3. – The parable of the rich man and Lazarus (16:19-31)

Jesus' story is about *a rich man who was dressed in purple and fine linen and lived in luxury every day* (19). But he isn't wise.

At his gate was laid a beggar named Lazarus, covered with sores (20): he is obviously in a bad way, because *even the dogs came and licked his sores* (21b).

But it looks like the rich man does nothing for this beggar, for Lazarus is *longing to eat from the rich man's table* (21a).

Both men die. Lazarus is carried *to Abraham's side* (22), which is picture language for what we might call heaven. The rich man, on the other hand, goes to *Hades, where he was in torment* (23a).

From where he is, the rich man can see *Abraham far away, with Lazarus by his side* (23b). Of course Jesus is not saying that this is possible in the afterlife: it's just a detail in the story.

So the man (he's not rich any more) asks Abraham to have pity on him and to *send Lazarus to dip the tip of his finger in water and cool my tongue, because I am in agony in this fire* (24).

But the answer is No, for two reasons.

The first is that what happens during our lives here on earth has eternal consequences. Abraham reminds him that *in your lifetime you received good things, while Lazarus received bad things, but now he is comforted here and you are in agony* (25).

It's like Abraham's saying *You never helped him; you weren't wise enough to use your worldly wealth to gain friends on earth so that you would be welcomed into eternal dwellings in heaven* (see verse 9).

The second reason Lazarus can't come from heaven to the suffering man in Hades is that *between us and you a great chasm has been set in place, so that those who want to go from here to you cannot, nor can anyone cross over from there to us* (26).

Now the man thinks that he can at least help his family to stop making the same mistake he made. So he begs Abraham to *send Lazarus to my family, for I have five brothers. Let him warn them, so that they will not also come to this place of torment* (27b-28).

Abraham's reply is that *they have Moses and the Prophets; let them listen to them* (29).

And when the man says that his brothers will repent *if someone from the dead goes to them* (30), Abraham replies *If they do not listen to Moses and the prophets, they will not be convinced even if someone rises from the dead* (31).

Here are the two most important lessons from the parable.

First, it really matters that we help those who are in need. Our decision has eternal consequences: people we help will one day welcome us in heaven (see verse 9). So it's the wise thing to do.

And second, wisdom comes from God's word (see also verses 16-17). In his parable Jesus is underlining the permanent value of the Old Testament: if people will not listen to Scripture, even a miracle will not convince them.

4. – Wisdom in the Jesus community (17:1-10)

Jesus assumes that all those who follow him will be in community together: he doesn't use the word *church*, but that's what he's talking about.

The citizens of the kingdom of God will want to be wise in the way they relate to one another.

Jesus makes four brief points.

First, the necessity of love (1-3a). Those who cause others to trip up, perhaps through unkindness or gossip, will be judged by God: *it would be* *better for them to be thrown into the sea with a millstone tied round their neck than to cause one of these little ones to stumble* (2).

In other words, a quick drowning would be a merciful alternative to the judgment coming their way.

So disciples need to make sure that they're loving one another. No wonder Jesus says *Watch yourselves* (3a).

Second, the importance of forgiveness (3b-4). *If your brother or sister sins against you, rebuke them* (3b). But the reason for doing this is so that they will repent. And Jesus says *If they repent, forgive them* (3c).

So forgiveness is not an optional extra in the Jesus community. However often someone sins against us and then repents, says Jesus, *You must forgive them* (4b).

Forgiving one another is the wise thing to do.

Third, the power of faith (5-6). The apostles ask Jesus *Increase our faith!* (5).

But it looks like Jesus is teaching here that that's not necessary: disciples can do extraordinary things *if you have faith as small as a mustard seed* (6).

So the cliché is true: what we need is not great faith in God, but faith in a great God. And faith grows as we see more and more how great God is.

Fourth, the danger of pride (7-10). If *one of you has a servant* (7a) who obeys orders, says Jesus, *will he thank the servant because he did what he was told to do?* (9).

We saw at the end of Part One of the Gospel that pride is a danger among the apostles: we heard them say *I am the greatest* and *We're the only ones* (see chapter 9:46-50).

So Jesus is saying that preening and complacency have no place in the disciple community.

Of course he will welcome us and even serve us (see Matt 25:23 and Luke 12:37), but pride has no justification. Jesus says to disciples *So you also, when you have done everything you were told to do, should say 'We are unworthy servants; we have only done our duty'* (10).

It would be good to take these four lessons for the Jesus community to heart: once again, it's the wise thing to do.

5. – Jesus heals ten lepers (17:11-19)

Should this incident be the beginning of Section Six, or here at the end of Section Five?

The reason for the question is that the *geographical marker* is here: chapter 17:11 begins *Now on his way to Jerusalem, Jesus...*

But the *important question* providing us with the theme for the new section doesn't appear until the beginning of the *next* incident: *Once, on being asked by the Pharisees when the kingdom of God would come...* (chapter 17:20a).

On balance I have thought it best to begin the new section at chapter 17:20. And, considering that the theme of the section we're just coming to the end of is *The Citizens of the Kingdom*, the incident *Jesus heals ten lepers* makes a great finish to Section Five.

Jesus is just about to enter a village, when ten men with leprosy call out to him: *Jesus, Master, have pity on us!* (13).

The healing is quickly described: Jesus tells them to show themselves to the priests and *as they went, they were cleansed* (14).

It looks like Luke is more interested, though, in what happens afterwards. One of the ten comes back, *praising God in a loud voice* (15). He throws himself at Jesus' feet and thanks him. Then Luke adds *And he was a Samaritan* (16b).

Jesus can hardly believe it. He asks *Where are the other nine? Has no one returned to give praise to God except this foreigner?* (18).

And he tells the man *Rise and go; your faith has made you well* (19).

The message of this incident is that we should be grateful for everything we've been given: wise people are quick to thank God.

But there is more. This is another story about an an outsider: the gratitude here is shown by a Samaritan rather than a Jew. The self-righteous in Israel reject the good news, while outsiders receive it: sinners, tax collectors, and Gentiles.

This ties this incident, at the end of Section Five, to Block A at its beginning. There we saw that Gentiles will take the places of some Jews at the messianic banquet (see chapter 13:28-30).

The good news of the kingdom of God is for Jews *and* Gentiles.

Learning the Gospel

I hope you will take the time to learn the order of the events in Section Five: it is not difficult and it is absolutely worthwhile.

Remember that the title of the section is *The Citizens of the Kingdom.* Now learn the headings of the three blocks (they're in bold): *Jews and Gentiles who count the cost / who know they were lost / and who want to live wisely.*

If you say these aloud a few times, they will soon be in your long-term memory.

Now go back to Block A. Repeat the titles of the five incidents until you can do it without looking: as you do it some of the details of each incident will come back to you.

Then go through the same process with Block B; and then with Block C.

You will find it easier to do all this if you have arranged with a friend to meet up after you have learnt Section Five.

I reckon you can learn the section in ten minutes. And it's worth it.

Section Five
The Citizens of the Kingdom

A. Jews and Gentiles who count the cost

1. The narrow door and the messianic banquet
2. Jesus' sorrow over Jerusalem
3. Jesus at a Pharisee's house
4. The parable of the great banquet
5. The cost of discipleship

B. ...who know they were lost

1. The Pharisees and the scribes
2. The parable of the lost sheep
3. The parable of the lost coin
4. The parable of the lost son
5. What happened to the older brother

C. ...and who want to live wisely

1. The parable of the wise manager
2. Jesus teaches about God's wisdom
3. The parable of the rich man and Lazarus
4. Wisdom in the Jesus community
5. Jesus heals ten lepers

Meeting the Lord

Once you have committed the structure to memory, start to tell the events of the section to yourself, or to a friend, including as many details as come to mind. As you do this, the Holy Spirit will be using the Jesus story in your life.

This will get you praying and worshipping too.

As you run through Block A in your mind, thank Jesus for his directness with the religious leaders about their refusal to respond to him. In Block B, thank God for his amazing grace in searching for and finding lost people like you. And in Block C you may want to ask God to give you wisdom to help you live your life *his* way and for *his* glory.

This is the Luke experiment: as you re-tell Luke you will be meeting the Lord.

Section Six: The Arrival of the Kingdom
Luke 17:20 – 19:27

We are still on the way to Jerusalem. In Section Four Jesus has taught his disciples how to live in the face of opposition to the message of the kingdom, while in Section Five he has described the characteristics of those who belong in the kingdom. Now, in Section Six, replying to a question as to when the kingdom of God will come, Jesus explains how his disciples are to live in the meantime.

Today salvation has come to this house,
because this man, too,
is a son of Abraham.
For the Son of Man came
to seek and to save the lost.

Luke 19:9-10

Enjoying the View

+ **Geographical marker:** *Now on his way to Jerusalem, Jesus travelled along the border between Samaria and Galilee (17:11).*
+ **Important question:** *Once, on being asked by the Pharisees when the kingdom of God would come, Jesus replied... (17:20).*

(For the significance of the *geographical marker* and the *important question*, see **Luke's Gospel: Part Two** on page 81.)

A. What to do till the kingdom comes (1) (17:20 – 18:17)

1. The kingdom of God is now (17:20-21)
2. The kingdom of God is coming (17:22-37)
3. The parable of the persistent widow (18:1-8)
4. The parable of the Pharisee and the tax collector (18:9-14)
5. Jesus and the little children (18:15-17)

B. What to do till the kingdom comes (2) (18:18 – 19:27)

1. Jesus and the rich ruler (18:18-30)
2. Third prediction (18:31-34)
3. Jesus heals a blind man (18:35-43)
4. Jesus calls Zacchaeus the tax collector (19:1-10)
5. The parable of the ten minas (19:11-27)

We are nearly in Jerusalem. In Section Six there is no opposition to Jesus, although he warns again that it is coming.

In both blocks here, Jesus is preparing his disciples for what is to come. He answers three questions: What is the kingdom going to look like? When is it going to arrive? And how are disciples to live in the meantime?

Please take a few minutes to read Luke's account from chapter 17:20 to chapter 19:27. Imagine the atmosphere as Jesus is approaching Jerusalem, and the questions people are asking.

And, as you do, talk to Jesus about what you're reading. Luke's Gospel is here so that we can *meet* him.

He wants to meet you, too.

Unpacking the Content

Luke reminds us with his geographical marker that Jesus is still on his way to Jerusalem (see chapter 17:11). Then some Pharisees ask him *when the kingdom of God would come* (see chapter 17:20).

The question sets the scene for Section Six.

A. What to do till the kingdom comes (1) (17:20 – 18:17)

1. – The kingdom of God is now (17:20-21)

The Pharisees assume that the kingdom is going to be a future event, but Jesus makes clear that it's *not something that can be observed* (20). It's not about saying one day *Here it is* or *There it is* (21a).

Because, says Jesus, the kingdom of God is now: it's *in your midst* (21b). It's about God's rule in human hearts, as people acknowledge Jesus as their king.

In other words, God's kingdom is already a reality, even if many people haven't noticed it (see chapter 11:20).

2. – The kingdom of God is coming (17:22-37)

Now Jesus is focusing on his disciples rather than on the Pharisees (see verse 22a). He tells them that the kingdom has a future element, too.

And he wants them to be ready.

Jesus now mentions *the day the Son of Man is revealed* (30): he's talking about himself. He *must suffer many things and be rejected by this generation* (25), but then one day he'll return to this world.

And that will be the final coming of the kingdom of God.

Jesus tells us three things about his return.

First, it will be unmistakeable (22-25). We are not to be fooled: when people say *There he is!* or *Here he is!* we should not believe them. The reason is that when Jesus returns it will be so obvious.

And he makes that clear: *The Son of Man in his day will be like the lightning which flashes and lights up the sky from one end to the other* (24).

No one is going to miss that.

Second, it will bring judgment (26-30). Jesus refers back to two examples of God's judgment in the Old Testament book of Genesis: the flood and the destruction of Sodom.

He is saying that judgment is going to come again.

In Noah's day and in Lot's day this was unexpected: *People were eating, drinking, marrying and being given in marriage* (27a; see also 28b). But *the day Noah entered the ark* (27b) and *the day Lot left Sodom* (29a), God's judgment fell on everyone else *and destroyed them all* (27c and 29c).

So Jesus' message is clear: *the day the Son of Man is revealed* (30b) will bring judgment with it.

So it's obvious what else we can say about Jesus' return.

Third, it will result in division (31-37). God's judgment is something we need to run from: *No one in the field should go back for anything* (31b).

Jesus spells out what will happen if we're living for ourselves: *Whoever tries to keep their life will lose it* (33a). But for those who give their lives to serve and follow Jesus there is good news: *Whoever loses their life will preserve it* (33b, and see chapter 9:24).

He is making it clear that there are two distinct groups of people: some will be waiting for his coming, and others won't. So *two women will be grinding corn together; one will be taken and the other left* (35; see also 34).

Jesus had told us at the beginning of Section Four's Block D that he had come to bring division (see chapter 12:49-53). We are either on his side or we're not.

It's not immediately clear what Jesus means with his proverb in verse 37. He may mean this: just as vultures spot a dead body and react accordingly, so we are to react accordingly when Jesus returns at the end of history.

In other words Jesus is saying *Be alert!*

3. – The parable of the persistent widow (18:1-8)

Now Jesus focuses on how disciples are to live in the present, before his return. The danger is that, because the wait is so long, they lose heart and sink into resignation.

So he tells a parable *to show them that they should always pray and not give up* (1).

There's an unjust judge, says Jesus: he *neither feared God nor cared what people thought* (2). And there's also a widow, which means that she has no support from husband or family: she begs the judge to *Grant me justice against my adversary* (3b).

And Jesus tells us something very important about her: she *kept coming* (3).

But the judge is not interested: *For some time he refused* (4a). But then he realises that the only way to stop the widow knocking on his door is to give her justice: *Even though I don't fear God or care what people think, yet because this widow keeps bothering me, I will see that she gets justice, so that she won't eventually come and attack me!* (4b-5).

And Jesus adds: *Listen to what the unjust judge says* (6).

Of course Jesus is not saying that God is like the judge. He is using a *how much more* argument. If this selfish scoundrel of a judge gives justice to the widow, how much more will God *bring about justice for his chosen ones, who cry out to him day and night?* (7).

Disciples of Jesus are God's *chosen ones* (7): he cares about them. So *he will see that they get justice, and quickly* (8a).

Before the parable began, Luke told us that Jesus was telling it so that disciples *should always pray and not give up* (1). After he has finished the story, Jesus concludes: *When the Son of Man comes, will he find faith on the earth?* (8b).

This links the parable with incident 2 in the block. When Jesus comes back in glory, will his disciples have the faith to have kept praying?

The message is clear: Jesus is telling us what to do as we await his return. We're to keep praying and to make sure the answer to his final question in verse 8 is *Yes*.

4. – The parable of the Pharisee and the tax collector (18:9-14)

Just as with the previous parable, Luke goes to the trouble of explaining to us *why* Jesus tells it: he's telling it to *some who were confident of their own righteousness and looked down on everyone else* (9; and compare verse 1).

The story overturns expectations.

When a Pharisee and a tax collector go up to the temple to pray, they both stand separate from the crowd. But for different reasons.

The Pharisee does it because he's *too good* to mix with others: *God, I thank you that I am not like other people [...] or even like this tax collector* (11). This is probably a genuine prayer, but we can still hear the smug self-congratulation.

The Pharisee adds that he keeps the religious rules: *I fast twice a week and give a tenth of all I get* (12).

The tax collector keeps his distance because he's *too bad* to mix with others. Instead of looking up to heaven he beats his breast and prays *God, have mercy on me, a sinner* (13b). Unlike the Pharisee, he knows he's a sinner and needs mercy from God: this looks like repentance.

And Jesus explains that *this man, rather than the other, went home justified before God* (14a). God sees the tax collector as being more righteous than the Pharisee: clearly he doesn't judge people by their behaviour, but by their heart attitude to him.

This overturns expectations. Jesus has already said this at the house of a prominent Pharisee (see chapter 14:11); now here he is, saying it again: *All those who exalt themselves will be humbled, and those who humble themselves will be exalted* (14b).

Between now and the return of Jesus in glory, disciples should not big themselves up, but realise that they depend always on the mercy of God.

5. – Jesus and the little children (18:15-17)

The disciples are not happy about people bringing babies to Jesus to be blessed: *they rebuked them* (15b).

But Jesus tells the disciples to let them through, and tells them why: *the kingdom of God belongs to such as these* (16b). Little children and babies, and anyone else seen as insignificant in first-century Jewish culture, will be welcomed into God's kingdom.

But there is more.

Jesus adds that *anyone who will not receive the kingdom of God like a little child will never enter it* (17). We will never be accepted by God unless we say goodbye to self-importance and are willing to be seen as insignificant.

Jesus has explained that the kingdom of God is now as well as future, and that both these aspects are intimately connected with him.

And if we have become part of the kingdom by starting to follow Jesus, we have learnt in Block A what we should be like while we are waiting for the kingdom's arrival in its fulness when Jesus returns in glory.

We must keep praying and stay humble.

But there is more to come.

B. What to do till the kingdom comes (2) (18:18 – 19:27)

This is the last block of five incidents before Jesus arrives in Jerusalem.

1. – Jesus and the rich ruler (18:18-30)

A certain ruler (we know that he's young: see Matt 19:20 and 22) asks Jesus *Good teacher, what must I do to inherit eternal life?* (18).

Jesus wants to show him that while the ambition (*eternal life*) is great, his understanding about how to get there (*What must I do..?*) is wrong. So he picks up on the fact that the ruler has addressed him as a *good teacher* (1): *Why do you call me good?* (19a).

Jesus tells the young man that *no one is good – except God alone* (19b). Because God is absolutely good, no human being can hope to reach him by doing deeds *they* think of as good.

Now Jesus takes him back to basics by saying *You know the command-ments* (20a) and listing five which are all concerned with right relationships with other people (see 20b).

The ruler's answer shows that he thinks righteousness is just about keeping the rules: he tells Jesus *All these I have kept since I was a boy* (21). He clearly thinks this is a test he's going to pass easily.

So Jesus goes further. He tells him to *sell everything you have and give to the poor* (22a). This is a test the man has not reckoned with. The question is: does he love God more than his wealth?

And Jesus is promising him *real* wealth if he puts God first: if he does all this he *will have treasure in heaven* and can follow Jesus (22b, and see chapter 12:33-34).

Luke tells us what happens next: the ruler *became very sad, because he was very wealthy* (23).

Now the man and those listening are going to learn the lesson: it is hard for rich people, says Jesus, to enter God's kingdom. To make the point clearer still, he adds that *it is easier for a camel to go through the eye of a needle than for someone who is rich to enter the kingdom of God* (25).

In other words: humanly speaking, it's impossible. That's because our pos-sessions can so easily take possession of us.

Understandably, people are asking *Who then can be saved?* (26). If not this man, who?

Jesus' answer offers hope to everyone: *What is impossible with man is pos-sible with God* (27).

The negative – and sad – example of the rich ruler has taught us something else about how disciples should live while waiting for the arrival of the kingdom with the return of Jesus.

Incident 1 urges us to ask ourselves what is more important to us: what we have or the one we follow.

2. – Third prediction (18:31-34)

With his geographical markers in Part Two of his Gospel, Luke has already told us that Jesus is on his way to Jerusalem (see chapter 9:51, 13:22 and 17:11).

But Jesus says it to the twelve disciples too: *We are going up to Jerusalem* (31a). The tension is increasing. The ultimate drama is soon to begin, because *everything that is written by the prophets about the Son of Man will be fulfilled* (31b).

Jesus is doubtless thinking of such prophecies as Isaiah 50:4-9 and Isaiah 52:13 – 53:12.

In this third prediction Jesus goes into more detail than in the first two about what will happen to him (compare chapter 9:22 and 9:43b-45).

Jesus says the Son of Man *will be handed over to the Gentiles* (32a). And he leaves the Twelve in no doubt as to what the Gentiles will do: *they will mock him, insult him and spit on him; they will flog him and kill him* (32b-33a).

Luke tells us that *the disciples did not understand any of this* (34a). The reason is that *its meaning was hidden from them, and they did not know what he was talking about* (34b).

Which presumably means that they didn't register the last thing Jesus had said about the Son of Man: *On the third day he will rise again* (33b).

So here is something else to do until the kingdom of God comes in its finality: Remember that the death and resurrection of Jesus are at the centre of God's purposes (see 31b).

3. – Jesus heals a blind man (18:35-43)

The blind man is *sitting by the roadside begging* (35). We know that his name is Bartimaeus if we've read Mark's Gospel (see Mark 10:46); but Luke chooses not to tell us this detail.

He is more interested in what the blind man calls Jesus: *Jesus, Son of David, have mercy on me!* (38).

This man seems somehow to have grasped that Jesus is the promised Messiah: the expression *Son of David* was often used in this way.

When people tell him to be quiet, *he shouted all the more 'Son of David, have mercy on me!'* (39b).

Now come some amazing words: *Jesus stopped* (40a). Jesus has time for a blind beggar, because he has time for everyone.

The blind man is brought to Jesus, who asks him *What do you want me to do for you?* (41a). And the answer comes: *Lord, I want to see* (41b).

Jesus tells him *Receive your sight; your faith has healed you* (42). And Luke adds that *immediately he received his sight and followed Jesus, praising God* (43a). It looks like this is much more than just a physical following.

This healed man has become a Jesus disciple.

The last sentence in incident 3 tells us that *when all the people saw it, they also praised God* (43b).

Maybe Luke is inviting us to join in. It's what disciples do.

4. – Jesus calls Zacchaeus the tax collector (19:1-10)

This incident completes a pair with the previous one: first Jesus heals a poor man, so that he starts to follow him, and now Jesus calls a rich man to join his team.

And there's a tension here. A few moments ago, in incident 1, we heard Jesus tell the rich ruler *How hard it is for the rich to enter the kingdom of God!* (see chapter 18:24).

And Zacchaeus is definitely rich: as a *chief tax collector* (2) he's collaborating with the Romans, who sold the task of collecting the taxes in a particular area to the highest bidder. There was little or no salary involved, so Zacchaeus was creaming off generous amounts of money for himself.

Luke tells us that *he wanted to see who Jesus was* (3a). That can't mean that Zacchaeus just wants to see what Jesus looks like. He's heard that Jesus has been transforming lives: is that where this curiosity comes from? Is he wishing the same thing could happen to him?

Because Zacchaeus is short and wants a decent view, *he ran ahead and climbed a sycamore-fig tree to see him* (4). So keen is he to see Jesus that he throws his dignity to the wind.

Maybe Zacchaeus is expecting to observe Jesus, not to encounter him. But Jesus stops, looks up, and says *Zacchaeus, come down immediately. I must stay at your house today* (5).

If Jesus knows his name, maybe he knows a lot more about him than that. So Zacchaeus *came down at once and welcomed him gladly* (6).

But not everyone is happy. The crowd starts to *mutter,* something that up to now in Luke's Gospel we've only heard the Pharisees and the scribes doing (see chapter 15:2). And it's the same complaint: Jesus *has gone to be the guest of a sinner* (7).

Their dismay is understandable: Jesus inviting himself to Zacchaeus' house shows a disregard for social norms. What *is* he thinking?

Zacchaeus makes his decision: *Look, Lord! Here and now I give half of my possessions to the poor, and if I have cheated anybody out of anything, I will pay back four times the amount* (8).

This is repentance. This is a fundamental change of heart and a determination to stop exploiting people (see chapter 3:12-13).

That's certainly the way Jesus sees it: he says *Today salvation has come to this house, because this man, too, is a son of Abraham* (9).

To some Jews, you were no longer part of God's chosen people if you worked as a tax collector for the Romans. But when Jesus sees the repentance Zacchaeus demonstrates, it's like he's saying *That's how I want my people to behave.*

And Jesus has one more thing to say. It's the climax of incident 4; in some ways it's the climax of the Gospel so far. He sums up his reason for coming into the world by telling us that *the Son of Man came to seek and to save the lost* (10).

Which brings us to incident 5.

5. – The parable of the ten minas (19:11-27)

Luke tells us that Jesus tells this parable *because he was near Jerusalem and the people thought that the kingdom of God was going to appear at once* (11b).

So the story will explain that there is going to be a period of time before the kingdom arrives in its fulness.

Most commentaries on Luke's Gospel suggest that this parable is a re-run of Jesus' parable of the servants given lots of money (often known as the parable of the talents): you can find it in Matthew 25:14-30.

So, they say, it's the same message. Jesus wants us to serve him with all the different gifts and resources he's given us. Then, on Judgment Day, we will be judged according to how we have used them.

Perhaps these commentaries are right. But I am uneasy about this, because there are elements in the parable of the ten minas which suggest that something different is going on here.

Here are two examples. Why do all the servants receive exactly the same amount of money? And why does Jesus tell us that the citizens in that country reject him?

Let's look at the first of those questions for a moment. If the servants are all those who say they want to serve Jesus, we know that we have *different* gifts, and some are more gifted than others.

But in the parable each servant is given one mina. What has Jesus given us that is the same for all of us? What do all servants of Jesus have, with no one having more than anyone else?

The answer is the gospel: *the good news of the kingdom of God* (see chapter 4:43).

Let's look at the parable in three stages, with that idea in mind.

Stage One (12-14). Jesus begins by telling us that *a man of noble birth went to a distant country to have himself appointed king and then to return* (12).

This is Jesus. At the end of Luke's Gospel, Jesus will ascend into heaven (see chapter 24:50-53); and the Old Testament prophecy of Daniel describes *one like a son of man, coming with the clouds of heaven* into God's presence, where he is *given authority, glory and sovereign power* (Dan 7:13-14).

But, Jesus tells us in the parable, *his subjects hated him and sent a delegation after him to say 'We don't want this man to be our king'* (14). Humanity has rejected Jesus; that's what sinners do.

So what does this man do before leaving to be appointed king? He *called ten of his servants and gave them ten minas* (13a). And he tells them to *put this money to work […] until I come back* (13b).

Jesus gives the gospel – *the good news of the kingdom of God* (4:43) – to each of his servants, and tells them to do what he has done: proclaim it.

Stage Two (15-26). One day the king returns and sends for his servants: he wants to find out what each has been doing with his mina (the gospel) while he has been away.

Jesus only tells us about three conversations the king has, but there are others: there are ten servants in the parable and Jesus has many who are apparently following him.

First, the king rewards the servants who have used what they had been given (see verses 16-19).

But then the king discovers that a third servant has never really known him at all: he has done nothing with his mina (the gospel) and has a wrong understanding of the king: *You are a hard man. You take out what you did not put in and reap what you did not sow* (21).

The king calls him a *wicked servant* (22a) and takes away from him what he has. He explains: *To everyone who has, more will be given, but as for the one who has nothing, even what they have will be taken away* (26, and see also chapter 8:18).

Stage Three (27). Jesus ends the parable by telling us what happens to the king's *subjects* who *hated him* (14): *Those enemies of mine who did not want me to be king over them – bring them here and kill them in front of me* (27).

There is a Judgment Day, when God's judgment will fall on all those who have not acknowledged Jesus as their king.

The parable of the minas is a fitting conclusion to Section Six of Luke's Gospel. What should Jesus' disciples be doing while they are waiting for the ultimate coming of the kingdom, when Jesus returns in glory?

We should be proclaiming the good news: Jesus is the Son of Man, who *came to seek and to save the lost* (see chapter 19:10).

We have reached a key moment in the Gospel. In chapter 9:51, at the start of Part Two, Jesus set out on a journey to Jerusalem, and the next thing we are going to read about is his arrival in the city. We have reached the end of Part Two.

In Part Three, Luke will tell us the end of the story.

Learning the Gospel

I hope you will take time to learn Section Six. Remember that this is not about learning every word but the order of the events.

First learn the two block titles in bold: you will find this extremely easy!

Then focus on Block A. Say the five incident titles aloud a few times, and they will soon be in your memory. As you learn them, many of the details of each incident will come back to you.

Then do the same with Block B.

Please remember that it will help to agree with a friend that you will both learn the structure of Section Six. Remember, too, that as more and more of the section gets into your memory, the Holy Spirit will use it to *change* you.

There is power in the word of God!

Section Six
The Arrival of the Kingdom

A. What to do till the kingdom comes (1)
1. The kingdom is now
2. The kingdom is coming
3. The parable of the persistent widow
4. The parable the Pharisee and the tax collector
5. Jesus and the little children

B. What to do till the kingdom comes (2)
1. Jesus and the rich ruler
2. Third prediction
3. Jesus heals a blind man
4. Jesus calls Zacchaeus the tax collector
5. The parable of the ten minas

Meeting the Lord

As you tell yourself (or your friend) the incidents of Block A, mentioning the details that come into your mind (and not worrying about those that don't), thank Jesus for the kingdom of God, and that one day he will return in glory.

Pray, too, that you will not give up praying, and that you will remember to be humble in the presence of God.

Then do the same with Block B. When you tell incident 1, ask Jesus to help you to love him more than anything else; in incident 2, thank him for his death and resurrection for you; in incidents 3 and 4 thank him that he came to seek and to save the lost.

And in incident 5, ask Jesus to help you proclaim the good news of the kingdom of God to people who don't yet know him.

And remember this: as you re-tell Luke you will rediscover Jesus.

Luke's Gospel
Part Three: The Climax

Chapter 19:28 – 24:53

Luke's central section (9:51 – 19:27) is finished:
Jesus is ready to enter Jerusalem.
So Part Three begins at chapter 19:28,
because we are arriving at **the climax** of the story.

In Part Three there are two sections:
once again, each contains
a number of blocks of five incidents each.

After an introduction in chapter 19:28-44,
Section Seven runs from 19:45 to 21:38
because the events Luke describes
all happen in the temple in Jerusalem
or just outside it.

Section Eight runs from 22:1 to 24:53.
It describes the end of the story:
Jesus' last supper with the disciples,
his praying in Gethsemane and his arrest there,
Peter's denial of Jesus, the trials,
and Jesus' crucifixion, death and burial.
The section ends with Luke telling us
about Jesus' resurrection appearances,
and then about his ascension.

So **Part Three: The Climax**
looks like this:

| Section Seven | 19:28 – 21:38 | Judgment on Israel |
| Section Eight | 22:1 – 24:53 | Jesus:
Saviour and King |

Section Seven: Judgment on Israel
Luke 19:28 – 21:38

At the beginning of Section Seven, Jesus, the promised Messiah, enters Jerusalem on a donkey and goes to the temple. The religious authorities are there: they continue their opposition and set traps for him with their questions. Jesus replies and asks questions of his own. Then, at the end of the section, he warns his disciples about God's judgment coming on Jerusalem, and specifically on the temple.

When Jesus entered the temple courts,
he began to drive out
those who were selling.

Luke 19:45

Enjoying the View

Introduction: Jesus arrives in Jerusalem (19:28-44)

A. Jesus debates with the religious leaders (19:45 – 20:40)

1. Jesus clears the temple (19:45-48)
2. The authority of Jesus questioned (20:1-8)
3. The parable of the tenants (20:9-19)
4. Paying taxes to Caesar (20:20-26)
5. Marriage at the resurrection (20:27-40)

B. Jesus announces God's judgment (20:41 – 21:38)

1. A question about the Messiah (20:41-44)
2. Warning about the scribes (20:45-47)
3. The widow's offering (21:1-4)
4. The destruction of the temple (21:5-33)
5. The end of all things (21:34-38)

Section Seven focuses on the confrontation between Jesus and the Jerusalem authorities: it begins with his arrival in the city.

After clearing the temple, Jesus spends the rest of Block A in discussion with the religious leaders: he answers their questions and he tells them a story.

In Block B it is Jesus doing all the talking (apart from chapter 21:7). For most of the block Jesus is teaching his disciples, preparing them for the time when he will no longer be with them.

Before reading further in this book, please read the whole section in Luke's. As you do, imagine the reactions of three groups to what Jesus does and says: the religious authorities, the crowds, and the disciples.

This is an essential part of the Luke experiment.

Unpacking the Content

Introduction: Jesus arrives in Jerusalem (19:28-44)

This introduction to Section Seven describes Jesus' journey to the point where he enters the temple, where the whole of Block A takes place.

First, what Jesus does (28-35). Throughout his ministry Jesus normally walked everywhere; now, for the only time, he is riding on a donkey. He has made careful preparations for this (see 29-34).

I don't know the reason Luke doesn't tell us why the donkey is important, because it looks like the crowds pick up on it, as we shall see. In the Old Testament prophecy of Zechariah we read *Say to your daughter Zion, 'See, your king comes to you, gentle and riding on a donkey'* (Zech 9:9).

This was recognised as referring to the Messiah. And now here is Jesus, deliberately fulfilling this prophecy. It's like he's arriving in Jerusalem holding a huge placard with the words on it *I am the Messiah!*

The two disciples who have collected the donkey *brought it to Jesus, threw their cloaks on it and put Jesus on it* (35).

Second, what the crowd shouts (36-38). As Jesus rides along *people spread their cloaks on the road* (36): this is what you did to show honour to a king (see 2 Kings 9:13).

Luke now tells us that *the whole crowd of disciples began joyfully to praise God* (37): it isn't the people of Jerusalem who are welcoming Jesus to their city, but many *disciples,* who remember *all the miracles they had seen* (37).

They are shouting *Blessed is the king who comes in the name of the Lord!* (38a): they are quoting the climax of the Hallel Psalms (113-118), which were chanted at all the great festivals of Israel (see Ps 118:26).

But they are adding the words *the king*: the messianic fervour is unmistakeable.

They are shouting something else too: *Peace in heaven and glory in the highest!* (38b), which will remind us of what the angels said when proclaiming the Messiah's birth to the shepherds (see chapter 2:14).

Third, what the Pharisees want (39-40). This is the last time Luke will mention the Pharisees: from now on Jesus' main opponents will be the Jerusalem religious leadership.

Some Pharisees tell Jesus to *rebuke your disciples* (39).

But for Jesus that is out of the question: *If they keep quiet, the stones will cry out* (40). Even inanimate creation understands what's happening here better than the Pharisees do.

But there is something else to see.

Fourth, why Jesus weeps (41-44). Now he is overcome with sorrow: *As he approached Jerusalem and saw the city, he wept over it* (41).

Jesus has already expressed his sadness about Jerusalem near the beginning of Section Five (see chapter 13:31-35), but now he is *weeping.*

Jerusalem was popularly understood to mean the place of peace (*shalom*): now Jesus is grieving because its people have not *known on this day what would bring you peace* (42).

But it looks like it's too late: *The days will come upon you when your enemies will build an embankment against you and encircle you and hem you in on every side* (43). Jesus' prophecy was fulfilled when the Romans laid siege to the city, leading to its devastation in AD70.

In chapter 13:35 Jesus has already prophesied that the temple will be destroyed; now he is talking about the fate of Jerusalem itself.

So, as he weeps, Jesus is warning of coming destruction: *They will dash you to the ground* [...]. *They will not leave one stone on another* (44a).

And the reason is clear: *You did not recognise the time of God's coming to you* (44b). Jesus already knows that whatever some individuals may decide, the city and its leadership will not recognise him as the Messiah.

Now, after this powerful introduction to Section Seven, Luke takes us into the temple for Block A.

A. Jesus debates with the religious leaders (19:45 – 20:40)

1. – Jesus clears the temple (19:45-48)

Jesus walks into the headquarters of first-century Jewish religion as if he owns the place (which he does).

He drives out *those who were selling* (45b), and explains his actions by quoting God's words from Old Testament prophecy: *My house will be a house of prayer* (46a, quoting Isaiah 56:7). But now, he says, it's *a den of robbers* (46b, quoting Jeremiah 7:11).

The people of God are supposed to be in relationship with God: talking to him should be central. But the temple now seems to be anything but *a house of prayer*.

We can only imagine how *the chief priests, the teachers of the law and the leaders among the people* (47b) are feeling because of what Jesus has said and done. Luke adds a note that *every day he was teaching at the temple* (47a), and that these leaders *were trying to kill him* (47b).

The reason they can't kill Jesus is that *all the people hung on his words* (48).

2. – The authority of Jesus questioned (20:1-8)

One day in the temple while Jesus is *proclaiming the good news* (1), *the chief priests and the teachers of the law, together with the elders* (1), ask him a question: *Tell us by what authority you are doing these things.* [...] *Who gave you this authority?* (2).

Jesus replies that he will answer their question if they will answer his. Here it is: *John's baptism – was it from heaven, or of human origin?* (3).

This is not a random question, because John the Baptist's baptism pointed forward to Jesus' own arrival on the scene. Saying that John's baptism was from God would mean acknowledging that Jesus' authority is from God, too.

So the religious leaders are in a quandary: if they say John's baptism was *from heaven,* Jesus will tell them that their unbelief is not logical (see 5).

But they can't say it was *of human origin* (6a), because, as they say to one another, *all the people will stone us, because they are persuaded that John was a prophet* (6b).

So they don't know which answer to give. There is only one option open to them: *We don't know where it was from* (7).

Well, says Jesus, *neither will I tell you by what authority I am doing these things* (8). Not a reply calculated to get his enemies to change their minds about him.

3. – The parable of the tenants (20:9-19)

This is the last parable Luke records Jesus as telling, and it is arguably his most important.

The vineyard is an Old Testament picture for the nation of Israel (see, for example, Isaiah 5:2). The man who *planted a vineyard, rented it to some farmers and went away for a long time* (9) is God: the tenants are the leaders of Israel.The servants he sends to the tenants *at harvest time* (10a) are the Old Testament prophets.

It's interesting *why* he sends them: it's *so they would give him some of the fruit* (10).

But instead of finding the qualities God expects to find in his people, his prophets were mistreated: one of them *they beat and treated shamefully and sent away empty-handed* (11). And when another was sent *they wounded him and threw him out* (12).

So Jesus tells us what the owner says: *What shall I do? I will send my son, whom I love; perhaps they will respect him* (13, and see chapter 3:22).

But when the tenants see the son they say to each other *This is the heir.* [...] *Let's kill him, and the inheritance will be ours* (14). There is something important to notice here: their argument only makes sense if the owner has died.

Whether his listeners get this or not, it's like Jesus is saying to them *You're behaving as if God were dead.*

So what do the tenants do to the owner's son? *They threw him out of the vineyard and killed him* (15a).

Jesus asks what the owner will do to those who have killed his son, and answers his own question: *He will come and kill those tenants and give the vineyard to others* (16a).

The people's response is *God forbid!* (16b). Is this because they have understood the implications of what Jesus is saying? Perhaps they realise that if the owner will *give the vineyard to others* (16a), that must mean a new leadership for a new Israel (see Matthew 21:43 for confirmation of this).

This new people of God is the church, made up of Jews *and* Gentiles who trust in Jesus the Son.

Jesus reinforces this by quoting from Psalm 118, as the crowds had in welcoming him to Jerusalem (see chapter 19:38a): *The stone the builders rejected has become the cornerstone* (17b, quoting Ps 118:22). And Luke tells us that, as he asked his question, *Jesus looked directly at them* (17a).

Do they understand what he's saying? Jesus is the stone rejected by the religious leader-builders, and this rejection will bring God's judgment down on them: *Everyone who falls on that stone will be broken to pieces; anyone on whom it falls will be crushed* (18).

Luke tells us that *the teachers of the law and the chief priests […] knew he had spoken this parable against them* (19). So they do get it. But, instead of repenting, they *looked for a way to arrest him immediately* (19).

4. – Paying taxes to Caesar (20:20-26)

The religious leaders send people *to catch Jesus in something he said* (20): Luke calls them *spies, who pretended to be sincere* (20a). The aim is to *hand him over to the power and authority of the governor* (20b).

After a heavy-handed display of flattery (see 21), they ask Jesus *Is it right for us to pay taxes to Caesar or not?* (22).

But Jesus is not fooled: *he saw through their duplicity* (23). He asks for a denarius coin and asks *Whose image and inscription are on it?* (24a).

When they answer *Caesar's* (24b), Jesus says *Then give back to Caesar what is Caesar's, and to God what is God's* (25).

Obviously this doesn't answer all the questions about Church and State, but the principle is clear: it's right to show allegiance to the state, but it's also true that allegiance to God matters.

Jesus may be saying something else here, too. Just as we owe the coin to Caesar because his image is on it, so we owe our *selves* to God, because his image is on us (see Gen 1:27 and James 3:9b).

Here are religious leaders who have never given themselves to God. No wonder that we read *Astonished by his answer, they became silent* (26).

5. – Marriage at the resurrection (20:27-40)

Now it's the Sadducees who have a question designed to trip Jesus up. It's about one of their favourite subjects: they don't believe there is life after death (see 27).

Their funny story is about a woman who marries seven brothers one after the other, according to the levirate law in the book of Deuteronomy (see 28-31, and Deut 25:5-6).

Then *the woman died too* (32).

So they ask Jesus *At the resurrection, whose wife will she be, since the seven were married to her?* (33).

In reply Jesus tells them two things.

First, he explains that there will be no marriage in heaven (see 35-36). And, second, because the Sadducees only accept the authority of the five books of Moses, he proves the reality of life after death from the book of Exodus.

Using the description of God at the burning bush (see 37, and Exod 3:6), Jesus concludes that God *is not the God of the dead, but of the living* (38).

Some of the scribes, hearing Jesus' reply to the Sadducees, say *Well said, teacher!* (39).

In Block A we have heard Jesus debating with the religious leadership of Israel: the tension is growing. And Luke adds that *no one dared to ask him any more questions* (40).

B. Jesus announces God's judgment (20:41 – 21:38)

The theme of judgment becomes more important in Block B. It's worth noticing that in Block B the religious leaders say nothing at all: this is no longer debate, it's *announcement.*

In incident 2, while still in the temple, Jesus warns that the scribes will be punished for their pride. And in incident 4 he points forward to God's judgment falling on Israel as a nation.

1. – A question about the Messiah (20:41-44)

Jesus asks the religious leaders a question. Why do they call the Messiah *the son of David,* when in the Psalms David refers to the Messiah as his *Lord?* (see 41-43, quoting Ps 110:1).

He asks the question directly: *David calls him 'Lord.' How then can he be his son?* (44).

The answer, of course, is that the Messiah is, in one person, the human son of David and the divine Lord of David. But Luke leaves us to work this out for ourselves.

2. – Warning about the scribes (20:45-47)

The scribes' job was to study and teach God's Law, but Jesus tells people to *beware of the teachers of the law* (46a).

There are two reasons.

First, they love honour. They *walk around in flowing robes and love to be greeted with respect in the market-places and have the most important seats in the synagogues and the places of honour at banquets* (46). For them being admired is what it's all about.

There's more: the scribes *make lengthy prayers*, and they do it *for a show* (47a): Jesus is saying that their religious activities are just about impressing others.

And second, they use others. Jesus says the scribes *devour widows' houses* (47a): does this mean they preyed on them by persuading them to part with their money for 'good causes'?

No wonder Jesus concludes that *these men will be punished most severely* (47b).

3. – The widow's offering (21:1-4)

Jesus sees rich people *putting their gifts into the temple treasury* (1). But then he sees *a poor widow put in two very small copper coins* (2).

The rich, says Jesus, are giving *out of their wealth* (4a), while the widow *out of her poverty put in all she had to live on* (4b).

So Jesus says that *this poor widow has put in more than all the others* (3). Of course, that's not true; but in God's way of reckoning, it is. For Jesus it's the devotion of the heart and the cost to the giver that count, rather than the amount of money.

This is the way God sees things, something Mary had made clear in her praise-prayer at the beginning of the Gospel (see chapter 1:51-53).

4. – The destruction of the temple (21:5-33)

At the start of the incident we read that *some of his disciples were remarking about how the temple was adorned with beautiful stones and with gifts dedicated to God* (5). The words *of his disciples* at the beginning of the sentence have been supplied by the translators, because Mark and Matthew make it clear that it was some disciples who broached the subject (see Mark 13:1-3 and Matt 24:1-3).

Jesus takes the opportunity to explain what is going to happen to the temple: he says that *the time will come when not one stone will be left on another; every one of them will be thrown down* (6, and compare chapter 19:44).

So the disciples ask the inevitable questions: *When will these things happen? And what will be the sign that they are about to take place?* (7).

There are four steps in Jesus' teaching here.

First, deceivers' lies (8-11). When there are *wars and uprisings* (9, and see verse 10), *earthquakes, famines and pestilences* (11), it will be easy to believe those who say the temple is about to be destroyed.

But, says Jesus, *do not follow them* (8b) and *do not be frightened* (9a). And he tells his disciples *why*: *These things must happen first, but the end* (of the temple) *will not come right away* (9b).

Second, disciples' persecution (12-19). *Before all this,* says Jesus, *they will seize you and persecute you* (12). Disciples will be arrested by Jewish authorities and by Gentile authorities, and all *on account of my name* (12).

And so, says Jesus, *you will bear testimony to me* (13).

They are not to worry about how they will defend themselves, *for I will give you words and wisdom that none of your adversaries will be able to resist or contradict* (15). Jesus will still be with his disciples when he is no longer physically present.

Disciples' persecution will include being betrayed by family and friends, *and they will put some of you to death* (16). This is strong language. And there is more to come: *Everyone will hate you because of me* (17).

But Jesus promises protection: *not a hair of your head will perish* (18). This cannot mean Jesus' disciples will never be harmed (see the previous paragraph); rather, they can have the assurance that any harm they suffer has been *permitted* by God their Father.

So persecution is going to come the disciples' way. But, says Jesus, *stand firm, and you will win life* (19).

Third, Jerusalem's trampling (20-24). The city is going to be *surrounded by armies* (20), and *Jerusalem will be trampled on by the Gentiles* (24b, and see chapter 19:43).

This prophecy was fulfilled when the Roman armies laid siege to Jerusalem. But, says Jesus, this will not just be a political event: it is a theological event too.

God will be using the armies of Rome as his judgment on Israel's spiritual rebellion: *this is the time of punishment* (22) and God's *wrath against this people* (23b).

Fourth, the temple's destruction (25-33). This is what Jesus' teaching has been leading up to: it is the answer to the disciples' questions back in verse 7.

There is apocalyptic language here: *signs in the sun, moon and stars* (25), *the heavenly bodies will be shaken* (26). But this is not talking about Jesus' return in glory at the end of human history, which he has already taught about in chapter 17:22-37.

Jesus is using apocalyptic language because, for the Jews, there could be nothing more appalling than the destruction of the temple: it would be like the whole world was falling apart.

Jesus says that *at that time they will see the Son of Man coming in a cloud with power and great glory* (27). This may sound to us like the Second Coming, but in fact it's almost certainly a reference to Jesus' exaltation as king.

We have already seen it. In the Old Testament prophecy of Daniel, the prophet sees *one like a son of man, coming with the clouds of heaven. He approached the Ancient of Days and was led into his presence* (Dan 7:13).

We've already seen it: this is not a coming *from* God, but a coming *to* God. This was fulfilled when Jesus, after his resurrection, ascended into heaven and returned to his Father.

Daniel goes on to say about the *one like a son of man* that *he was given authority, glory and sovereign power; all nations and peoples of every language worshipped him* (Dan 7:14).

My view is that this is what Jesus is talking about here in Luke chapter 21. When the temple is destroyed this will be a visible sign of judgment, and will show that Jesus is the glorious Son of Man in his Father's presence.

When you see all these things happening, Jesus adds, *you know that the kingdom of God is near* (31). And he uses a fig-tree as an example (see 29-30).

That this is all about the destruction of the temple (and not about Jesus' Second Coming) is confirmed by these words of Jesus: *This generation will certainly not pass away until all these things have happened* (32).

And Jesus is very sure that his teaching about the temple's destruction is true: *Heaven and earth will pass away, but my words will never pass away* (33).

5. – The end of all things (34-38)

There is no clear change of topic in verse 34, but at this point in Matthew and Mark's chapters about the destruction of the temple, Jesus starts teaching now about his own glorious return at the end of human history (see Matt 24:35-36 and Mark 13:31-32).

Hence the heading I have given to incident 5.

Certainly Jesus' words in verse 34 will remind us of chapter 17:26-35, where he is certainly talking about his Second Coming. And what Jesus is talking about here in incident 5 doesn't just apply to Israel: *it will come on all those who live on the face of the whole earth* (35).

So disciples are to *watch* and *pray* [...] that we may *be able to stand before the Son of Man* on Judgment Day (36).

Judgment has been one of the main themes of Section Seven, as Jesus has taught for several days (see 37). And people wanted to hear Jesus teaching: they *came early in the morning to hear him in the temple* (38).

Learning the Gospel

I hope you will take the time to learn the order of the incidents in Section Seven: it won't take you long because there are only two blocks.

First, learn the two block headings, which are in bold. Saying them aloud will make this much easier.

Now focus on Block A. Say the five incident titles several times, and keep saying them until you can do it without looking at your Bible or at *The Luke Experiment.*

Then do the same with Block B.

Remember that agreeing with a friend that you will both do this will make it easier.

Section Seven
Judgment on Israel

Introduction: Jesus arrives in Jerusalem

A. Jesus debates with the religious leaders
>   1. Jesus clears the temple
>   2. The authority of Jesus questioned
>   3. The parable of the tenants
>   4. Paying taxes to Caesar
>   5. Marriage at the resurrection

B. Jesus announces God's judgment
>   1. A question about the Messiah
>   2. Warning about the scribes
>   3. The widow's offering
>   4. The destruction of the temple
>   5. The end of all things

Meeting the Lord

As you tell yourself the section incident by incident, including as many details as occur to you, talk to the Lord, too, about what you are hearing in his teaching. The purpose of Luke's Gospel is not only that we get information about Jesus, but also that we get to know him better.

So let me encourage you to spend time with him as you work your way through the section.

And remember that doing this with a friend is fun, and worthwhile too: you will help one another and grow together in your love for Jesus.

This is the Luke experiment: as you re-tell Luke, you will rediscover Jesus.

Section Eight: Jesus: Saviour and King
Luke 22:1 – 24:53

The whole Gospel has been leading up to this secrtion: now we are reaching the climax of the story Luke has to tell. In Section Eight we will meet betrayal, anguish, confusion, fear and despair, but most of all we will see love. We will see the depth of Jesus' love at the cross, its triumph at the empty tomb, and its glory at his ascension. This is holy ground.

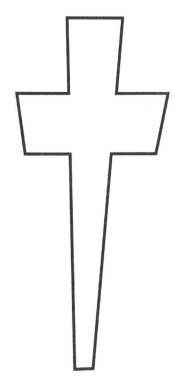

When they came
to the place called the Skull,
they crucified him there.

Luke 23:33a

Enjoying the View

A. Jesus: teaching and alone (22:1-53)

1. Plans against Jesus (22:1-6)
2. The last supper (22:7-23)
3. Jesus teaches after the supper (22:24-38)
4. Jesus prays on the Mount of Olives (22:39-46)
5. Jesus arrested (22:47-53)

B. Jesus: condemned and crucified (22:54 – 23:56)

1. Peter denies Jesus (22:54-62)
2. The four trials (22:63 – 23:25)
3. The crucifixion (23:26-43)
4. The death of Jesus (23:44-49)
5. The burial of Jesus (23:50-56)

C. Jesus: risen and ascended (24:1-53)

1. The women meet the angels at the empty tomb (24:1-8)
2. Peter at the empty tomb (24:9-12)
3. The road to Emmaus (24:13-35)
4. Jesus appears to all the disciples (24:36-49)
5. The ascension of Jesus (24:50-53)

Section Eight has three blocks, each containing five incidents. This makes it easy to memorise the order of events.

If we take Block B, with its description of the cross, as the centre of everything, then Block A is *before* and Block C is *after*. In Block A Jesus prepares the disciples for what is going to happen and prepares himself for the suffering awaiting him, while in Block C we meet the risen Jesus and see him ascend into heaven.

Please take time to read through Section Eight in Luke's Gospel in one sitting: you may even like to read it aloud. Much of it will be familiar. But try to imagine the scene and the emotions of all those who have anything to do with Jesus.

As you read, you may find yourself stopping to worship.

A. Jesus: teaching and alone (22:1-53)

1. – Plans against Jesus (22:1-6)

Most people are in Jerusalem to celebrate Passover: to thank God for rescuing Israel from slavery in Egypt. But the religious leaders have something else on their minds: *the chief priests and the teachers of the law were looking for some way to get rid of Jesus* (2).

But they have to be careful, because *they were afraid of the people* (2b).

The chief priests and the officers of the temple guard (4a) have a visitor: Judas, who Luke reminds us is *one of the Twelve* (3), goes and *discussed with them how he might betray Jesus* (4b).

Luke tells us something else too. This betrayal offer was prompted by the fact that *Satan entered Judas* (3).

So the deal is done. *They were delighted and agreed to give him money* (5), and Judas *consented, and watched for an opportunity to hand Jesus over to them when no crowd was present* (6).

2. – The last supper (22:7-23)

Luke tells us that we are approaching the day on which *the Passover lamb had to be sacrificed* (7), and shows us that Jesus has gone to great lengths to make the practical arrangements for the meal (see 8-13).

As the supper begins, Jesus tells the apostles that he has *eagerly desired to eat this Passover with you before I suffer* (15): is this because he knows that the bread and wine will explain the meaning of his death?

At every Passover, four cups of wine were shared before, during and after the meal: the words said with each cup helped everyone look *back* to God's rescue of Israel.

Luke tells us about the second and third Passover cups (see 17 and 20): the words Jesus speaks over the third help his disciples look *forward* to his death and its meaning.

They must already realise that Jesus is soon going to leave them: he tells them at the start of the meal that *I will not eat it again until it finds fulfilment in the kingdom of God* (16, and see also 18). He is referring to the messianic banquet (see my comments on chapter 9:10-17).

During the supper Jesus gives bread to his disciples with the words *This is my body given for you; do this in remembrance of me* (19).

Then, after the supper, it is time for the third cup of the Passover meal. Jesus' words are significant: *This cup is the new covenant in my blood, which is poured out for you* (20).

There were Old Testament promises that God would one day establish a new covenant in which men and women would find forgiveness in a relationship with God (see Jer 31:31-34) and experience the presence of the Holy Spirit living in them (see Ezek 36:26-27).

Now Jesus is saying that his death will make that covenant reality in the lives of all who become his disciples: his blood is going to be poured out *for you* (20b).

It looks like Jesus goes straight on to say that not everyone present is really in relationship with him: *the hand of him who is going to betray me is with mine on the table* (21). Jesus adds that *the Son of Man will go as it has been decreed. But woe to that man who betrays him!* (22).

So the disciples, understandably, *began to question among themselves which of them it might be who would do this* (23).

3. – Jesus teaches after the supper (22:24-38)

Now that the supper is over, there is time for Jesus to prepare his friends for what is to come. He knows their unspoken thoughts and he knows what they need to hear.

From what Jesus says here we can see that the disciples are asking themselves four questions.

First: Who's the greatest? (24-27). This question is audible: *A dispute also arose among them as to which of them was considered to be the greatest* (24).

Jesus reminds the disciples that *the kings of the Gentiles lord it over them* (25a). But, he adds, *you are not to be like that* (26a).

So Jesus is turning the world upside down: *the one who rules* should be *like the one who serves* (26b).

He spells it out with a question of his own: *For who is greater, the one who is at the table or the one who serves? Is it not the one who is at the table?* (27a).

Then he adds *But I am among you as one who serves* (27; see also chapter 12:37).

When the disciples asked *Who's the greatest?* they were looking for a name. But Jesus is saying that the greatest is *the one who serves* (27b).

Second: What's going to happen to us? (28-30). His friends, says Jesus, *have stood by me in my trials* (28).

But in the future Jesus will *confer on you a kingdom, just as my Father conferred one on me* (29). Which will mean two things for the disciples.

The first is that they will celebrate with him at the messianic banquet: they will *eat and drink at my table in my kingdom* (30a). And the second is that they will *sit on thrones, judging the twelve tribes of Israel* (30b).

The disciples' future is in good hands.

Third: How are we going to cope? (31-34). Jesus tells his friends that *Satan has asked to sift all of you as wheat* (31): he wants them to desert Jesus.

But Jesus has prayed for Peter (interestingly, he calls him *Simon* here) *that your faith may not fail* (32a). And he adds that, after Peter is on his feet again, he should *strengthen your brothers* (32b).

This is reassurance for the disciples: they will cope with tough circumstances because of Jesus' prayers and Peter's leadership.

But Peter is sure that he will never let Jesus down: he is willing to *go with you to prison and to death* (33). But Jesus gives him a stark warning: *Peter, before the cock crows today, you will deny three times that you know me* (34).

Fourth: How is the kingdom going to come? (35-38). Jesus reminds the disciples of the way God looked after them when they were out on their mission (see 35 and chapter 9:1-6).

But now, in verse 36, he tells them to buy swords. This must surely be meant ironically: Jesus must be wanting them to see that violence is not going to bring the kingdom in. When the disciples say *See, Lord, here are two swords,* Jesus closes down the conversation by replying *That's enough!* (38).

So what *is* going to bring in the kingdom of God?

Jesus quotes from the fourth Servant Song in the Old Testament prophecy of Isaiah: *And he was numbered with the transgressors* (37a, quoting Isa 53:12). This is the song which teaches that the Servant of the Lord is *crushed for our iniquities; the punishment that brought us peace was on him* (Isa 53:5).

And now Jesus says to his friends *I tell you that this must be fulfilled in me* (37b). So important is this, that he says it again: *Yes, what is written about me is reaching its fulfilment* (37c).

In other words, Jesus is saying *I am the Servant of the Lord, who will give his life to set sinners free.* (See also my comments on chapter 14:16-17.)

The kingdom of God will be brought in not by disciples' swords, but by the Servant's death.

In his teaching after the last supper, Jesus is preparing his disciples for what is to come.

4. – Jesus prays on the Mount of Olives (22:39-46)

Jesus takes the disciples to the Mount of Olives: he needs to pray. *On reaching the place,* says Luke (40a), he spoke to them. Because we've read Mark's Gospel, we know that the place is a garden called Gethsemane (see Mark 14:32).

After telling the disciples to *pray that you will not fall into temptation* (40b), Jesus moves away *a stone's throw beyond them, knelt down and prayed* (41). His body language speaks volumes.

Jesus prays *Father, if you are willing, take this cup from me* (42a): the cup is a picture of God's punishment for sin (see, for example, Isaiah 51:17). Jesus is shrinking from what lies before him: not simply from the physical pain, but also from the spiritual cost. He will take the divine judgment onto himself which others deserve.

But through it all Jesus remains in submission to his Father: *Yet not my will, but yours be done* (42b).

Luke doesn't tell us that Jesus spent three extended times of prayer, but he does tell us this: *Being in anguish, he prayed more earnestly, and his sweat was like drops of blood falling to the ground* (44, and see Heb 5:7).

Jesus fears the cross.

Returning to the disciples, Jesus finds them asleep, *exhausted from sorrow* (45b). He wakes them and urges them to *pray that you will not fall into temptation* (46b, and see 40).

5. – Jesus arrested (22:47-53)

Luke wants to emphasize how alone Jesus is: Judas is *one of the Twelve* (47a). He arrives in Gethsemane with a crowd of armed men (47).

When Judas makes to kiss him, Jesus asks *Are you betraying the Son of Man with a kiss?* (48).

There are so many other ways Judas could have pointed Jesus out to the arresting party. But he chooses a sign of love.

In response to Jesus' imminent arrest, the disciples resort to violence in order to engineer an escape (see 49). And, when the right ear of the high priest's servant is cut off, Jesus puts a stop to the rescue attempt: *'No more of this!'* Luke adds that *he touched the man's ear and healed him* (51, and see John 18:10).

Jesus asks *the chief priests, the officers of the temple guard, and the elders* why they are arresting him as if he is *leading a rebellion* (52): when he had been teaching in the temple courts *you did not lay a hand on me* (53a).

Then he says to them *But this is your hour – when darkness reigns* (53b).

With his Block A Luke has shown us how alone Jesus is: his friends don't understand him and his enemies hate him. But he explains his upcoming death to the disciples and prepares them for what is to come.

B. Jesus: condemned and crucified (22:54 – 23:56)

1. – Peter denies Jesus (22:54-62)

After the last supper Jesus had told Peter *Before the cock crows today, you will deny three times that you know me* (see chapter 22:34). And in Gethsemane Jesus had told the disciples to *pray that you will not fall into temptation* (see chapter 22:40 and 46).

But Peter has not taken the warning to heart. After Jesus' arrest, he has been sitting in the courtyard outside the high priest's house, where Jesus is being held. But three times he claims not to have any connection with him (see 57, 58 and 60).

The third time, *just as he was speaking, the cock crowed. The Lord turned and looked straight at Peter* (60b-61a).

Then Peter remembers *the word the Lord had spoken to him* (61b). So *he went outside and wept bitterly* (62).

2. – The four trials (22:63 – 23:25)

Luke tells us that *the men who were guarding Jesus began mocking and beating him* (63).

If Jesus were really a prophet he would be able to know people's identity even when he can't see them. So *they blindfolded him and demanded 'Prophesy! Who hit you?'* (64).

And Luke adds that *they said many other insulting things to him* (65).

And now the interrogations begin: they may not all be official trials, but in all of them Jesus is being cross-examined.

And a verdict is being reached.

There are four distinct stages. Only in the first two does Jesus say anything.

First, before the Jewish Council (22:66-71). The Council consists of *the elders, […] the chief priests and the teachers of the law* (66). They want to know what Jesus is claiming about himself.

If you are the Messiah, they say, *tell us* (67a).

Jesus replies that they're not going to believe him anyway. He adds *But from now on, the Son of Man will be seated at the right hand of the mighty God* (69).

This is incendiary stuff. Jesus is clearly claiming to be the glorious Son of Man of the prophecy of Daniel (see Dan 7:13-14), sitting at the right hand of God (see Ps 110:1). They may think they are getting rid of Jesus, but they will soon see his authority established and, by implication, their own destroyed.

They may succeed in having him killed, but his execution will be the beginning, not the end.

There is a second question: *Are you then the Son of God?* (70a). With his reply *You say that I am* (70b) Jesus is saying that he is, but that he disagrees with their understanding of exactly what that means.

But he has said enough for the Jewish Council. They say *Why do we need any more testimony? We have heard it from his own lips* (71). Anyone claiming to be the Son of God and to share God's heavenly authority is dangerous.

So they take him to the Roman governor.

Second, before Pilate (23:1-7). The Jews had no power to carry out a death sentence, so there is no alternative.

The leaders of *the whole assembly* (1) bring their charges against Jesus in a way designed to worry Pilate: *He opposes payment of taxes to Caesar and claims to be Messiah, a king* (2).

The first accusation is wrong. The second should concern a Roman governor, as it suggests that Jesus has political ambitions.

So Pilate asks Jesus *Are you the king of the Jews?* (3a).

Once again, Jesus replies *You have said so* (3b, and see chapter 22:70). His answer is non-committal.

For Jesus, the common Jewish understanding of the Messiah (or king of the Jews), that he would throw the Romans out of Israel, is simply wrong (see my comments on chapter 9:21).

Doubtless Pilate will have questioned Jesus further, but he reaches a conclusion. He tells the chief priests and the crowd *I find no basis for a charge against this man* (4).

He sees no grounds for the accusations against Jesus.

But the religious leaders are not giving up. They tell Pilate that Jesus *stirs up the people* and that *he started in Galilee and has come all the way here* (5).

But their mention of Galilee gives Pilate an opportunity. He can buy time, and possibly support, by sending Jesus to the ruler of Galilee, Herod Antipas (see 6-7).

Third, before Herod (23:8-12). Herod was nominally Jewish: it looks like he has come to Jerusalem for the Passover feast.

Luke has already told us that Herod is curious about Jesus (see chapter 9:7-9, but see also chapter 13:31-33). But now he is to meet him for himself.

Herod may well see Jesus as a kind of magician: *He hoped to see him perform a sign of some sort* (8). *He plied him with many questions, but Jesus gave him no answer* (9). To such a person Jesus has nothing to say.

After the religious leaders set about accusing Jesus (see 10), *Herod and his soldiers ridiculed and mocked him. Dressing him in an elegant robe, they sent him back to Pilate* (11). Herod is frustrated: he has not got what he was looking for.

Luke adds: *That day Herod and Pilate became friends* (12a), probably because Herod agrees with Pilate that there is no reason to sentence Jesus to death (see 15).

So there is a fourth and final stage in these trials.

Fourth, before Pilate again (13-25). The governor calls *the chief priests, the rulers and the people* (13) and tells them that he has *found no basis for your charges against him* (14b), and that Herod agrees (see 15).

So Pilate has made his decision about Jesus: *He has done nothing to deserve death. Therefore, I will punish him and then release him* (15b-16). By *punish* Pilate means that he will have Jesus whipped.

This is probably Pilate's way of trying to satisfy the Jewish leaders, short of actually having Jesus executed.

But the crowd are still not giving up. Luke doesn't mention the tradition that a prisoner would be released every year at Passover, but that is the reason for the shouting: *Away with this man! Release Barabbas to us!* (18).

So they are choosing Barabbas (who Luke tells us is a terrorist and a murderer, see 19) over Jesus. And when Pilate tries again, they keep shouting *Crucify him!* (21).

Despite yet another attempt by Pilate to avoid the inevitable, Luke tells us that the pressure from the crowds wins the day: *their shouts prevailed* (23b).

So Pilate gives way. He releases Barabbas, and *surrendered Jesus to their will* (25).

Jesus has been condemned to death.

3. – The crucifixion (23:26-43)

Jesus will be crucified in verse 33. Before this, Luke mentions three individuals or groups who are involved in some way as Jesus is being led out. And after the crucifixion itself, as he is hanging on the cross, we meet three groups again.

All of which is an invitation to us to decide how *we* are going to respond to the crucified God.

First, before the crucifixion (26-31). *The soldiers led him away* (26a), but it looks like Jesus no longer has the strength to carry the crossbeam (the upright was probably already at the site of execution).

So *they seized Simon from Cyrene, who was on his way in from the country, and put the cross on him* (26). Simon is in the wrong place at the wrong time. But the fact that we know his name (and those of his two sons, see Mark 15:21), suggests that he may have been so impacted by all this that he became a disciple of Jesus.

Luke may even imply that by mentioning that they put the cross on to Simon and made him carry it *behind Jesus* (26b). Jesus himself had said that anyone wanting to be his disciple must *take up their cross daily and follow me* (chapter 9:23, and see 14:27). So Simon is already following Jesus (he's behind him) before he starts following him as a disciple.

Some of the women from Jerusalem are being impacted by Jesus' suffering, too: they *mourned and wailed for him* (27).

It looks like Jesus stops to speak to them. He tells them *Do not weep for me; weep for yourselves and for your children* (28). What happens to

Jerusalem will affect them much more seriously than what is happening to him (see verses 29-31).

After Simon from Cyrene and the *daughters of Jerusalem* (28a), Luke also tells us that *two other men, both criminals, were also led out with him to be executed* (32). We will learn more about them after Jesus has been nailed onto his cross.

Second, the crucifixion itself (33-34). *When they came to the place called the Skull, they crucified him there* (33a).

There is no description of what this involves: perhaps most of Luke's first readers would be familiar with the details, even if they had never witnessed a crucifixion.

The other Gospels call the place *Golgotha*, but Luke translates the word from Aramaic to Greek so that his Gentile readers can understand it: it's *the place called the Skull* (33a).

As Jesus is being crucified, he prays. Not for himself, but for the soldiers: *Father, forgive them, for they do not know what they are doing* (34). They certainly don't care: they cast lots to decide who is going to get his clothes.

Jesus is right: the soldiers *do not know what they are doing* (34). They are crucifying the Son of God.

So Jesus is now up on the cross. And Luke reminds us that the criminals are there too: *one on his right, the other on his left* (33b).

Third, after the crucifixion (35-43). *The people stood watching* (35a), but Luke mentions three groups involved in some way in what they are witnessing.

The religious leaders are sneering (see chapter 16:14), apparently enjoying the show: *He saved others; let him save himself if he is God's Messiah, the Chosen One* (35b). The truth, of course, is somewhat different: it is *in order* to save others that he is not saving himself.

The soldiers are mocking Jesus. They've seen the notice above his head reading *This is the King of the Jews* (38); they offer him wine vinegar (an act of cruelty), and say *If you are the king of the Jews, save yourself* (37).

And the third group Luke mentions as Jesus is hanging on his cross is the two criminals again.

One of them *hurled insults at him: 'Aren't you the Messiah? Save yourself and us!'* (39).

But the other criminal *rebuked him* (40a), and then says something extraordinary: *We are punished justly, for we are getting what our deeds deserve. But this man has done nothing wrong* (41).

What he knows about himself is that he's guilty. What he knows about Jesus is that he's innocent.

This looks like repentance and faith. He calls out *Jesus, remember me when you come into your kingdom* (42), and Jesus has good news for him: *Today you will be with me in paradise* (43).

We've seen how different people have been impacted by the crucifixion of Jesus. You might want to take this opportunity to tell God how you feel, and what you believe, about the cross of Jesus.

And to worship him.

4. – The death of Jesus (23:44-49)

Now Luke tells us about three hours of darkness (see 44): is he wanting us to remember that darkness was the last plague in Egypt before the Passover lambs were killed (see Exod 10:21-23)?

Then we're told that *the curtain of the temple was torn in two* (45b). The curtain before the holy of holies kept temple worshippers out of the presence of God: their sin made access into his presence impossible.

But now the curtain has gone, because Jesus is about to die. With the tearing of the curtain, God is saying to anyone who will listen *You can come in now!*

Jesus prays a last prayer: *Father, into your hands I commit my spirit* (46a). Then Luke tells us *When he had said this, he breathed his last* (46b).

But there is more to say about Jesus' death. The centurion, who presumably has been present at many crucifixions, *praised God and said 'Surely this was a righteous man'* (47). He has never witnessed a crucifixion like this: he realises that something supernatural is happening here.

The crowd *beat their breasts and went away* (48), but not those who have got to know Jesus: they *stood at a distance, watching these things* (49b). And Luke specifically mentions *the women who had followed him from Galilee* (49, and see chapter 8:1-3).

They are soon going to play a vital role in what happens after the Sabbath.

5. – The burial of Jesus (23:50-56)

Joseph, *from the Judean town of Arimathea* (51b), is *a member of the Council, a good and upright man* (50).

It looks like he had been overruled when the Jewish Council had met, because *he had not consented to their decision and action* (51a).

And, most important of all, he is *waiting for the kingdom of God* (51c): this is Luke's way of telling us that Joseph is a secret disciple of Jesus (see Matthew 27:57).

He goes to Pilate and *asked for Jesus' body* (52). He is outing himself as a Jesus follower. Luke may be encouraging us to do the same.

Joseph takes the body down from the cross, *wrapped it in linen cloth and placed it in a tomb cut in the rock, one in which no one had yet been laid* (53). *It was Preparation Day* (54), which means it was Friday: the burial has to be completed before the Sabbath begins at sunset.

Now Luke returns to *the women who had come with Jesus from Galilee* (55). After seeing where the tomb is, they go home *and prepared spices and perfumes* (56).

This means two things. They love Jesus, and they are expecting that he is going to stay dead.

C. Jesus: risen and ascended (24:1-53)

Of the final block of five incidents, four are about the resurrection of Jesus. (For a brilliant treatment of the various accounts in the four Gospels, I recommend John W. Wenham, *Easter Enigma: Do the Resurrection stories contradict one another?* Paternoster Press 1984.)

1. – The women meet the angels at the empty tomb (24:1-8)

Early on Sunday morning, the women (see chapter 23:55a) go to the tomb, taking their spices with them.

But they get a shock: *they found the stone rolled away from the tomb, but when they entered, they did not find the body of the Lord Jesus* (2-3).

Now another shock: *Suddenly two men in clothes that gleamed like lightning stood beside them* (4). The mention of the brightness of lightning indicates that something supernatural is happening here (see chapter 9:29), and the women, perhaps after the event, realise that the *two men* are, in fact, *angels* (see verse 23).

The women are terrified. The angels say *Why do you look for the living among the dead? He is not here; he has risen!* (5b-6a), and remind them that Jesus had said he would be crucified *and on the third day be raised again* (7).

And now it all comes back to them: *Then they remembered his words* (8).

2. – Peter at the empty tomb (24:9-12)

The women hurry back to tell their story *to the Eleven and to all the others* (9). The overwhelming reaction is that *they did not believe the women, because their words seemed to them like nonsense* (11).

But maybe Peter wonders if there might just be something in it. In any case *he got up and ran to the tomb* (12a). There's no angel, but *he saw the strips of linen lying by themselves* (12b).

So, says Luke, *he went away, wondering to himself what had happened* (12c).

3. – The road to Emmaus (24:13-35)

Incident 3 grips the imagination. Two disciples are walking from Jerusalem to a village called Emmaus. We know the name of one of them: Cleopas (see verse 18).

These disciples go through four stages as the story unfolds.

First, they meet a stranger (13-18). Understandably, they are *talking with each other about everything that had happened* (14).

Then, says Luke, *Jesus himself came up and walked along with them; but they were kept from recognising him* (15b-16).

When he asks what they're talking about, *they stood still* (17b): are they just so surprised by the question? In any case, Cleopas asks a question of his own: *Are you the only one visiting Jerusalem who does not know the things that have happened there in these days?* (18).

Everything is set for stage two.

Second, they tell their story (19-24). When the stranger asks *What things?* (19a), the floodgates open: they tell their story about *Jesus of Nazareth* (19a).

They talk about his identity: *He was a prophet, powerful in word and deed before God and all the people* (19b).

They talk about his death: *The chief priests and our rulers handed him over to be sentenced to death, and they crucified him* (20). And this means that their belief that Jesus might have been the Messiah has died too: *We had hoped that he was the one who was going to redeem Israel* (21).

And they tell the stranger about his resurrection, or at least about what others have said about this. The women went to the tomb, *but didn't find his body* (23a), and then claimed they had *seen a vision of angels, who said he was alive* (23b).

And then some of their friends had gone to the tomb and found it empty: *but they did not see Jesus* (24b).

Cleopas and his companion are in disarray: sad and confused. But the stranger has something for them.

Third, they hear his teaching (25-27). The stranger tells them that they are *slow to believe all that the prophets have spoken* (25). And he asks another question: *Did not the Messiah have to suffer these things and then enter his glory?* (26).

He answers his own question. The stranger *explained to them what was said in all the Scriptures concerning* the Messiah (27).

I wonder how long this lasted. How long did Jesus talk for? Which parts of Scripture did he quote and explain? All we can be sure of is that he showed these two disciples – from the Jewish Scriptures – that the Messiah *had* to suffer, die and rise again.

I bet they were listening. But there is more to come.

Fourth, they meet the Lord (28-32). The two disciples urge the stranger to stay with them in Emmaus, because *the day is almost over* (29).

When they sit down to eat, the guest suddenly becomes the host: *he took bread, gave thanks, broke it and began to give it to them* (30).

And in that moment it happens: *their eyes were opened and they recognised him, and he disappeared from their sight* (31).

They know that it's all true: Jesus is the Messiah, the hope of Israel, and he has risen from the dead. And they discover they had both had the same experience while listening to the stranger's teaching: *Were not our hearts burning within us while he talked with us on the road and opened the Scriptures to us?* (32).

The rest of the story is quickly told. The two disciples rush back to the others in Jerusalem, but before they can say what's happened to *them*, they are told the news: *It is true! The Lord has risen and has appeared to Simon* (34).

The joy that must have filled the disciples that day can be ours, too.

4. – Jesus appears to all the disciples (24:36-49)

While they were still talking about this, says Luke, *Jesus himself stood among them* (36a). They are *startled and frightened* (37), so it's no wonder that Jesus says to them *Peace be with you* (36b).

There are two aspects to what happens here.

First, confirmation (37-43). Jesus wants to convince the disciples that he has really risen from the dead. So he tells them to *look at my hands and my feet* (39a): the marks of crucifixion will have been unmistakeable. This really was their friend who had died on a cross.

And he invites them to *touch me* (39b): if they do, they will see that he has a real body and so cannot be a ghost.

After showing the disciples *his hands and feet* (40), he asks for something to eat (see 41b), not because he's hungry but in order to show that his body is real. He takes the piece of broiled fish they give him and he *ate it in their presence* (43).

When Jesus had first appeared to them, the disciples *did not believe it because of joy and amazement* (41a): it was all too good to be true.

But Jesus has confirmed that the message of the resurrection – and therefore the whole good news of the kingdom of God – is true.

But he has something else for them.

Second, commissioning (44-49). It looks like Jesus repeats for all the disciples at least some of what he had said to the two disciples on the road to Emmaus (see verses 25-27).

He *opened their minds so they could understand the Scriptures* (45), and he sums up the core message like this: *The Messiah will suffer and rise from the dead on the third day* (46).

But Scripture also teaches, says Jesus, that *repentance for the forgiveness of sins will be preached in his name to all nations, beginning at Jerusalem* (47). The message is that people who repent of their sin will be forgiven by God, and it's for Jews (*beginning at Jerusalem*) and for Gentiles (*to all nations*).

So the disciples are going to do this preaching. And for two reasons. They have seen all this happen: they are *witnesses of these things* (48); and they are going to be equipped through being *clothed with power from on high* (49).

Jesus is talking about the gift of the Holy Spirit, who will be poured out on the Church: this, says Jesus, is *what my Father has promised* (49).

So, having confirmed to the disciples that the message is true, the risen Jesus is going to send them out to preach it. The good news of the kingdom of God (see chapter 4:43) is *for the world.*

5. – The ascension of Jesus (24:50-53)

As Jesus ascends to go back to his Father, he is blessing all his disciples. This is the last memory they have of him: he is the risen Lord who blesses all those who follow him.

There are some who say that the ascension is *a made-up story* which shows what *the Church* thinks of Jesus: they are wrong. In fact the ascension is *a historical event* which shows what *God the Father* thinks of Jesus.

Luke gives us a fuller account of the ascension at the beginning of his second book (see Acts 1:4-11) and tells us what happened afterwards *on earth*, while Daniel in his prophecy tells us what happened afterwards *in heaven* (see Dan 7:13-14).

So Jesus *left them and was taken up into heaven* (51b). But the disciples are not sad, because they have the promise that they are soon going to be *clothed with power* (see 49b).

Instead *they worshipped him and returned to Jerusalem with great joy* (52). We should notice how they feel about Jesus: they are *worshipping* him.

As we reach the end of Luke's Gospel, it would be good for us to do that, too.

Learning the Gospel

Section Eight is easy to learn: I hope you will take the time to do it.

First, learn the three block headings, which are in bold: doing this aloud makes the whole thing much quicker.

Then go back to Block A. Say the five incident headings several times, until you know them without looking at your Bible or at *The Luke Experiment.* This really isn't difficult, as most of us know the order of the events in this part of the Gospel story fairly well already.

Now do the same with Block B, and then with Block C.

And remember that you will enjoy this more if you have arranged with a friend that you will both do this.

I am praying that you will enjoy learning Section Eight of Luke's Gospel.

Section Eight
Jesus: Saviour and King

A. Jesus: teaching and alone
1. Plans against Jesus
2. The last supper
3. Jesus teaches after the supper
4. Jesus prays on the Mount of Olives
5. Jesus arrested

B. Jesus: condemned and crucified
1. Peter denies Jesus
2. The four trials
3. The crucifixion
4. The death of Jesus
5. The burial of Jesus

C. Jesus: risen and ascended
1. The women meet the angels at the empty tomb
2. Peter at the empty tomb
3. The road to Emmaus
4. Jesus appears to all the disciples
5. The ascension of Jesus

Meeting the Lord

As you move through the events of Section Eight in your mind, or with a friend, stop and thank Jesus for his love at every step of the way. Ask him to make these events real to you; ask him to touch your heart with his love.

Thank Jesus for what he has done for you: for forgiveness and reconciliation with God through his cross, and for new life and new hope through his resurrection.

Tell God you want to be someone who takes every opportunity he gives, to share the good news of the gospel, and open yourself up again to the power of the Holy Spirit, who lives in you.

And *worship* Jesus: he is seated at the right hand of God the Father.

My Conclusion:
The Experiment goes on

I hope you have taken time on your way through *The Luke Experiment* to learn the structure of the Gospel.

In Section One Luke was *introducing Jesus*: you saw him call people to follow him and do extraordinary miracles; at the beginning of Section Two Jesus called twelve apostles: you watched them *experiencing Jesus* through his powerful works and powerful teaching; and in Section Three you saw the apostles *recognising Jesus* as the Messiah and the Son of God.

In Section Four you watched as Jesus equipped his disciples to face *the opposition to the kingdom*; in Section Five you listened to Jesus explaining what *the citizens of the kingdom* are like; and in Section Six you heard him talking about how disciples should live between now and *the arrival of the kingdom*.

In Section Seven you watched as Jesus arrived in Jerusalem and went to the temple to tell the religious leaders about God's *judgment on Israel*; and in Section Eight you saw Jesus explaining his death to his disciples and going to the cross as our *saviour and friend*.

You also saw disciples meeting the risen Jesus and heard him commission them to spread the message of the gospel in the power of the Holy Spirit. And you watched as he ascended out of their sight, back to his Father.

And, whether you have learnt and used the structure or not, I hope you have been rediscovering Jesus.

But that process doesn't need to stop because you have reached the end of this book. I want to suggest a few ways in which you can keep using Luke's Gospel to help you get to know Jesus better.

1. Using Luke's Gospel for worship and prayer

Take one section of Luke. As you begin to run through it in your mind (without your Bible), don't just remember the order of the incidents in each block: talk to Jesus about what he is doing and saying. Enjoy spending time with him. Worship him for his power and his love. And pray for yourself as you think your way through the section.

You can do this at home in your room, or while you are sitting on the bus. You might decide to use Section One this way for a week; the following week you could move on to Section Two.

2. Using Luke's Gospel to help you pray for others

Sometimes you want to pray for a friend or a family member, but you're not sure how. Why not take one section of the Gospel and pray through it, praying the whole time for this particular person?

With some incidents you will be praying that she will recognise more and more who Jesus is and why he came; sometimes you will be praying that she will understand more fully what it means to follow Jesus; sometimes you will be praying that she will decide to give her life in service for him.

Luke's Gospel can help us pray for others, whether these people are already Christians or not.

3. Using Luke's Gospel for a Luke Walk

Go for a walk (without a Bible) with a friend who has learnt the same section(s) of Luke as you have. Take turns to tell each other the incidents, including as many details as you can remember. This is not a competition: you can help one another as you re-tell Luke.

When you get home you might take some time to thank Jesus and worship him together. (You might also want to turn to Luke's Gospel to remind yourselves of any details neither of you could remember.)

The Luke Walk works well with a group too. But however you do it, it is so healthy to be using Luke's Gospel to help you get to know Jesus better.

4. Using Luke's Gospel in a teaching programme

Your youth group or student group might decide to use the structure of Luke in its term programme. At your first meeting you could look at Luke's Introduction, at your second meeting Section One, and so on.

Obviously you won't be able to cover every detail. But different small groups could look at different parts of the section, before each group shares with everyone else what they've learnt.

And some of the small groups might decide to learn the structure of the week's section for themselves, so they can use it in the week to come.

This could work well, too, in a church's Sunday teaching programme. The first sermon in a series could be on chapters 1 and 2 (Luke's Introduction). Then you could have one or two sermons on each section in turn.

Of course this will be more of an overview than a detailed study of every incident. But sometimes, in the longer Bible books where we often get lost, an overview is exactly what we need.

5. Using Luke's Gospel in a small group

It is possible to study the whole of Luke's Gospel – and to learn it too – in a church home group or in some other kind of small group. There are suggested outlines for such a series in Appendix 2.

Finally...

Thank you for reading *The Luke Experiment.*

Being a Christian is about much more than just knowing lots about Jesus. Once we have turned from our sin and trusted him, it's about *encounter*: getting to know him better.

The Holy Spirit uses all kinds of things to help us to grow. But I am convinced of this: what he uses more than anything else to help us to know Jesus better is the Bible.

Please pray for yourself, and for others trying the Luke experiment, that all of us will love and experience Jesus more. That's what disciples do.

This will make us want to help others to be his disciples, too.

Appendix 1:
Questions about Luke's Gospel

Below are some of the questions I have most often been asked while I've been writing this book. I can only comment briefly here: see the larger commentaries for more details.

1. Who says Luke's Gospel has a structure at all?

I can't prove that it has, but it seems to me to make sense.

In a culture in which you couldn't print off copies of books, it strikes me that writing with a memorable structure is the obvious thing to do.

As Luke was writing something he considered incredibly important, he wanted people to pass it on to others: if they could learn the order of all the incidents off by heart, that's exactly what they could do.

2. What are the main views about Luke's structure?

Older commentaries tend to have a section in their Introduction called *Structure,* but most modern commentaries have opted out, and call that section *Outline* or sometimes *Analysis*: it's a list of the incidents.

However, what nearly all commentaries agree on is that chapter 9:51 to chapter 19:27 is Luke's central section or travel narrative: Jesus is on a journey from Galilee to Jerusalem (it's what I call *Part Two* in this book). The commentaries then group the incidents into thematic clusters.

But apart from acknowledging the central section, most scholars, it seems to me, don't really think Luke's Gospel has a structure at all.

My problem with that is that learning the order of the events will prove difficult, if not impossible.

None of the commentaries I have looked at considers the value of *learnability* in the first century (see Question 1, above).

And perhaps they are right.

3. Who says my structure of Luke's Gospel is the right one?

Well, certainly not me.

There are a great many suggested analyses of Luke, and it's a brave Bible teacher who claims they have found *the* right one.

But what I am saying about this structure is that it's *regular*: all the sections, and Luke's Introduction too, contain blocks of five incidents. And that means it's easier to learn. It has not been difficult for me to learn all the incidents in order.

If my structure of Luke's Gospel is not *Luke's* structure of his Gospel, that doesn't bother me. I am not using this structure to teach some weird and wonderful new doctrine: if you've read the book you've seen that what I'm trying to do is simply teach through Luke's Gospel.

And in such a way that you can commit it to memory.

4. What is the relationship between Luke's Gospel and the Gospels of Matthew and Mark?

The issue of the order in which these three Gospels were written (known as the synoptic problem) is reckoned to be one of the most complicated in all literature: I make no claim to have studied this topic in detail.

The majority of scholars think that Mark's Gospel was written first, and that Matthew and Luke used and expanded Mark.

That may well be the case. But it is worth mentioning that this is far from proven.

For what it is worth, my guess is that Matthew wrote his Gospel before Mark, and then Luke, wrote theirs.

But I have written *The Luke Experiment* without a particular solution to the synoptic problem in mind.

5. What is my favourite commentary on Luke?

I have learnt from a number of Luke commentaries, including those by William Taylor and Darrell Bock.

I am very grateful to William Taylor, in his two *Read, Mark, Learn* volumes on Luke's Gospel, for pointing out the role of the geographical markers and important questions in what I call *Part Two* of Luke (see page 81). This doesn't mean that I agree with him on the structure of Luke as a whole, but his insight with the markers and questions in chapter 9:51 – 19:27 is extraordinarily helpful: I have found it nowhere else.

But the commentary I am most impressed by and have used most is Dick France's in the *Teach the Text* series. He is not much interested in Luke's structure, but he is always biblical, thorough and clear. I experience joy whenever I read one of his books.

R. T. France, *Luke,* Baker Books 2013.

Appendix 2:
The Luke Experiment in a Small Group

The following series of studies has 10 sessions and is designed for group use; but of course you could also use these questions on your own or one-to-one with a friend.

These studies are meant for people who have already read the relevant section in *The Luke Experiment.* In a home group context it might make sense if everyone reads the whole section in Luke's Gospel before coming to the meeting: this will save significant time.

One possible way of doing these studies in a group is to divide into pairs: each pair looks at one part of the passage and tries to answer the questions. After 10 minutes, each pair shares what they have learnt and the group talk about it.

It is up to you whether you combine answering the questions with learning the structure!

10 Weeks in Luke's Gospel

Week One
Luke's Introduction
(Luke chapters 1 and 2)

Look at Luke's title page: Chapter 1:1-4

1. Why do we think Luke decided to write his Gospel? And how did he go about it?

Look at Block A: Chapter 1:5-80

2. Why do we think God goes to so much trouble announcing John's birth and then making it happen?

3. Let's try to describe Mary's different feelings in verses 29, 34 and 38. What do we think is the most important thing Gabriel tells her about the baby she's going to have?

4. What does Zechariah say about God in his outburst of praise in verses 68-79?

Look at Block B: Chapter 2:1-52

5. Do we think the shepherds will have understood the message of the angels in verses 10-14? What is there in the passage that demonstrates this?

6. Let's look at Simeon and Anna in the temple. Why does Simeon decide to praise God? And why does Anna decide to tell a particular group of people about Jesus?

7. When Jesus is with the teachers in the temple in verse 46, why do we think he's asking questions? Is there any evidence here that he knows his true identity?

8. As we look back on these first two chapters of Luke's Gospel, let's make a list together of some of the things we have learnt about Jesus.

Do any of us know Luke's Introduction by heart? Would any of us like to?

Week Two
Section One: Introducing Jesus
(Luke 3:1 – 6:11)

Look at Block A: Chapter 3:1 – 4:30

1. In what way do we think John prepares the way for Jesus? What does he say in his preaching that tells us what he is hoping to achieve?

2. Which experience do we think was harder for Jesus: his temptation by Satan or his preaching in the synagogue in Nazareth? Why?

Look at Block B: Chapter 4:31 – 5:16

3. If Luke knows Mark's Gospel, he deliberately adds the story of Jesus calling the first disciples (chapter 5:1-11). Why do we think Luke thinks this incident is so important?

4. What parts of these incidents demonstrate the extraordinary authority of Jesus? And why does he say he's come?

Look at Block C: Chapter 5:17 – 6:11

5. Why do we think the Pharisees and the scribes are so against Jesus? What reasons will have been most important for them?

6. Let's make a list of everything Jesus says in Block C about who he is. Do we think the crowds understood all his claims? And what about the religious leaders?

Look at the whole of Section One: Chapter 3:1 – 6:11

7. If we could have been in the crowd to witness one of these events, which would we choose? And why?

8. If we each had to pick out one thing Jesus says from the whole of Section One, which would we choose? Why?

Do any of us know the incidents of Section One by heart? Would any of us like to?

Week Three
Section Two: Experiencing Jesus
(Luke 6:12 – 8:56)

Look at the Introduction and Block A: Chapter 6:12-49

1. Why do we think Jesus spends the night praying before choosing the twelve apostles? Why is this such a big decision?

2. What part of Jesus' teaching in his sermon in chapter 6 is the hardest to put into practice? And the easiest?

Look at Block B: Chapter 7:1 – 8:3

3. Let's try to find some ways in which Jesus demonstrates his authority in Block B. Why will Jesus' teaching in incident 4 have been hard for Simon the Pharisee to hear?

4. There are quite a number of women involved in the incidents here. What does this tell us about Jesus?

Look at Block C: Chapter 8:4-21

5. The parable of the sower teaches us that not everyone will respond positively to Jesus. Do we find this parable encouraging or discouraging?

6. Block C is very short. What do we think the main lesson is that Luke wants us to learn? How will we know if we've learnt it or not?

Look at Block D: Chapter 8:22-56

7. Which miracle here do we think demonstrates Jesus' power most? Why?

8. Let's look at the way different people react to the four miracles here. Why the differences? Who do we think we are most like?

Do any of us know the incidents of Section Two by heart? Would any of us like to?

Week Four
Section Three: Recognising Jesus
(Luke 9:1-50)

Look at the Introduction to the section: Chapter 9:1-6

1. Luke doesn't tell us anything about how the apostles' training mission went. So why does he bother telling us about it?

Look at Block A: Chapter 9:7-27

2. What do we think the most important incidents are here? Why do we think each individual incident matters?

3. Why do we think Jesus starts talking about discipleship when he does? What's the connection with what's gone before?

4. Why do we think Jesus wants the disciples to recognise that he's the Messiah? What do we think convinced them?

Look at Block B: Chapter 9:28-50

5. Why do we think Jesus only took Peter, James and John up the mountain to witness his transfiguration? Let's make a list of what they *should* have learnt from the experience. Do we think they did?

6. What do we think the strengths and weaknesses of the disciples are in Block B? Does Luke put more emphasis on their strengths or their weaknesses?

7. When Jesus predicts his death for a second time, why do we think God prevents them from understanding this? And why do we think they are afraid to ask Jesus what he means?

8. Let's look back at both blocks. What evidence is there that it makes any difference to the disciples that they recognise that Jesus is the Messiah and the Son of God?

Do any of us know the incidents of Section Three by heart? Would any of us like to?

Week Five
Section Four: The Opposition to the Kingdom
(Luke 9:51 – 13:21)

Look at Block A: Chapter 9:51 – 10:37

1. Jesus gets some opposition from Samaritans at the beginning of the block. What does Jesus think about Samaritans? What can we learn from this?

2. How might we describe Jesus' attitude to potential disciples? And his relationship with his Father?

Look at Block B: Chapter 10:38 – 11:36

3. Why is it much easier for us to be like Martha than like Mary? How do we think we can change?

4. Block B has some things we can do when faced with opposition to the gospel. What strikes each of us as the most important?

Look at Block C: Chapter 11:37 – 12:48

5. What lessons in incidents 2 and 4 are the most important for each of us? Why? How are we going to put this into practice?

6. Thinking about the parable of the rich fool, why do we naturally think that getting bigger barns is going to make our lives better? When we think that way, what are we forgetting?

Look at Block D: Chapter 12:49 – 13:21

7. What three things do we need to do in order to make sure we're really part of the Jesus team? Which is the hardest for us? And the most important? Why?

8. Jesus promises division *and* growth in the kingdom of God. Which of these motivates each of us most to keep following Jesus? Why?

Do any of us know the incidents of Section Four by heart? Would any of us like to?

Week Six
Section Five: The Citizens of the Kingdom
(Luke 13:22 – 17:19)

Look at Block A: Chapter 13:22 – 14:35

1. What does Jesus say in Block A about Gentiles being invited into the kingdom of God? What is his attitude to his own people the Jews?

2. Do we think that what Jesus says about the cost of discipleship is a bit over the top? Why or why not? What helps us to be willing to decide to follow Jesus?

Look at Block B: Chapter 15:1-32

3. What does Jesus want the Pharisees and the scribes to learn from these three parables? Do we think they did? Why or Why not?

4. In what way were all of us lost before God found us? How does the parable of the lost son help us to understand what God is like?

Look at Block C: Chapter 16:1 – 17:19

5. Can we try to put in our own words in what sense the wise manager is a good example for us? What could that mean in practice?

6. Let's look at the rest of Block C. Which incident do we think is the most important? How do we think Jesus is wanting us as his disciples to respond to the block? What's that going to mean for us in practice?

Look at the whole of Section Five: Chapter 13:22 – 17:19

7. Which of these fifteen incidents is the most important for each of us, and why? And which is the most irritating or disturbing, and why?

8. If we see ourselves as citizens of the kingdom of God, how do we want to pray that God will change us so we can follow Jesus more faithfully?

Do any of us know the incidents of Section Five by heart? Would any of us like to?

Week Seven
Section Six: The Arrival of the Kingdom
(Luke 17:20 – 19:27)

Look at Block A: Chapter 17:20 – 18:17

1. In what way is it true that the kingdom of God is now, and in what way is it true that it's coming? Which of these do we think is more important?

2. Jesus is teaching here about how his disciples should live while they are waiting for the arrival of the kingdom in its fulness. Which lesson does each of us think is the most important, and why?

3. What have we not understood if we think that God is like the unjust judge in the parable in incident 3?

4. And what have we not understood if we feel proud that we're more like the tax collector than the Pharisee?

Look at Block B: Chapter 18:18 – 19:27

5. Let's look at Jesus and the rich ruler in incident 1. Where has the topic of attitude to possessions already come up in Luke's Gospel? Why do we think it appears again now?

6. Do we think Andrew's understanding of the parable of the ten minas is right, or do we think it's a bit far-fetched? Why? What lesson do we think Jesus wants us to learn?

7. Let's look at chapter 19 verse 10. Why does this really fit here, at the end of the Zacchaeus story? What other examples of this have we already seen in Luke's Gospel? And in what way has each of us experienced the truth of this?

8. How do we think we should be waiting for the arrival of God's kingdom in its fulness?

Do any of us know the incidents of Section Six by heart? Would any of us like to?

Week Eight
Section Seven: Judgment on Israel
(Luke 19:28 – 21:38)

Look at the Introduction: Chapter 19:28-44

1. What words might we use to describe Jesus in this passage? What emotions might he be experiencing as he rides into Jerusalem? Why?

Look at Block A: Chapter 19:45 – 20:40

2. Which of the incidents here do we think will have made the religious leaders most angry? Why?

3. How do we think Jesus is feeling when he tells the parable of the tenants? Why?

4. How would we describe Jesus' attitude towards the leaders of Israel?

Look at Block B: Chapter 20:41 – 21:38

5. Do we think the religious leaders understand what Jesus is getting at with his question about the Messaih (incident 1)?

6. Let's look at what Jesus says about the destruction of the temple in chapter 21:5-33. Do we think the disciples are encouraged or discouraged as they hear Jesus say this?

7. Do we agree with Andrew that Jesus changes the subject in chapter 21:34 and starts talking about the end of all things? Or is he still talking about the temple being destroyed?

Look at the whole of Section Seven: Chapter 19:28 – 21:38

8. Jesus must have known that his teaching in these chapters is going to make the religious leaders more determined than ever to get rid of him. So why does he talk like this?

Do any of us know the incidents of Section Seven by heart? Would any of us like to?

Week Nine
Section Eight – Jesus: Saviour and King
(Luke 22:1 – 24:53)

Look at Block A: Chapter 22:1-53

1. What do we think the main things are that the disciples learn at the last supper? Which might be the most important?

2. Can we spot different ways in which Jesus' aloneness is underlined here in Block A? What do we think the main reasons are that Jesus decides in Gethsemane to do his Father's will?

Look at Block B: Chapter 22:54 – 23:56

3. Let's think about what Andrew calls the four trials. How would we describe Pilate's attitude to Jesus? Why does Jesus say nothing in the third and fourth trials?

4. Let's think about the various groups impacted by Jesus' crucifixion. Which affects each of us most? Why?

5. How do we think Luke wants us to respond to Jesus' death? And in what way is Joseph of Arimathea an example for us?

Look at Block C: Chapter 24:1-53

6. Which of these resurrection appearance stories grabs us most? Why?

7. Why do we think Luke tells us the story of Jesus appearing to the whole group of disciples in incident 4? What do we think is the most important thing he says to them?

8. Why do we think Luke adds the story of Jesus' ascension? The other Gospel writers don't do this, so why is it so important to Luke?

Do any of us know the incidents of Section Seven by heart? Would any of us like to?

Week Ten
Review of Luke's Gospel

1. Let's all take two minutes to look through the Gospel and pick moments which are highlights for us. Then share in the whole group.

2. Why might we invite a younger Christian to read through Luke's Gospel with us?

3. And why might we invite a friend who's not a Christian to read through Luke's Gospel with us?

4. Let's keep our Bibles open as we pray together. Let's thank God for as many things in Luke's Gospel as we can think of, and ask him to help us to be faithful followers of Jesus.

Do any of us know the structure of the whole of Luke's Gospel by heart? Would any of us like to?

Appendix 3:
The Structure of Luke's Gospel

Luke's Introduction (Luke 1:1 – 2:52)

Luke's title page (1:1-4)

A. Before the birth of Jesus (1:5-80)

1. The birth of John the Baptist announced (1:5-25)
2. The birth of Jesus announced (1:26-38)
3. Mary visits Elizabeth (1:39-56)
4. The birth of John the Baptist (1:57-66)
5. Zechariah prophesies and praises God (1:67-80)

B. The birth and boyhood of Jesus (2:1-52)

1. The birth of Jesus (2:1-7)
2. What the angel says (2:8-21)
3. What Simeon says (2:22-35)
4. What Anna says (2:36-40)
5. The boyhood of Jesus (2:41-52)

Part One: The King (3:1 – 9:50)

Section One
Introducing Jesus (3:1 – 6:11)

A. The foundation of Jesus' ministry (3:1 – 4:30)

1. John: his identity and message (3:1-20)
2. Jesus: his baptism (3:21-22)
3. Jesus: his genealogy (3:23-38)
4. Jesus: his temptation (4:1-13)
5. Jesus: his identity and message (4:14-30)

B. The beginning of Jesus' ministry (4:31 – 5:16)

1. Jesus drives out an evil spirit (4:31-37)
2. Jesus heals Simon's mother-in-law and others (4:38-41)
3. Jesus says his priority is preaching (4:42-44)
4. Jesus calls the first disciples (5:1-11)
5. Jesus heals a leper (5:12-16)

C. The opposition to Jesus' ministry (5:17 – 6:11)

1. Jesus forgives and heals a paralysed man (5:17-26)
2. Jesus calls Levi and eats with sinners (5:27-32)
3. Jesus predicts a radical break with Judaism (5:33-39)
4. Jesus is Lord of the Sabbath (6:1-5)
5. Jesus provokes opposition by healing on the Sabbath (6:6-11)

Section Two
Experiencing Jesus (6:12 – 8:56)

Introduction: Jesus chooses the twelve apostles (6:12-16)

A. The disciples of Jesus (6:17-49)

1. Blessings and woes (6:20-26)
2. Love your enemies (6:27-36)
3. Don't judge others (6:37-42)
4. A tree and its fruit (6:43-45)
5. The wise and foolish builders (6:46-49)

B. The authority of Jesus (7:1 – 8:3)

1. Jesus heals a centurion's servant (7:1-10)
2. Jesus raises a widow's son from death (7:11-17)
3. Jesus and John the Baptist (7:18-35)
4. Jesus is anointed by a sinful woman (7:36-50)
5. Jesus' team includes many women (8:1-3)

C. The teaching of Jesus (8:4-21)

1. The parable of the sower (8:4-8)
2. Jesus explains why he teaches in parables (8:9-10)
3. Jesus explains the parable of the sower (8:11-15)
4. The parable of the lamp (8:16-18)
5. Jesus' true family (8:19-21)

D. The power of Jesus (8:22-56)

1. Jesus calms a storm (8:22-25)
2. Jesus drives out Legion (8:26-39)
3. Jesus meets Jairus (8:40-42a)
4. Jesus heals a sick woman (8:42b-48)
5. Jesus raises Jairus' daughter from death (8:49-56)

Section Three
Recognising Jesus (9:1-50)

Introduction: Jesus sends out the twelve apostles (9:1-6)

A. Jesus is the Messiah (9:7-27)

1. Herod: his question (9:7-9)
2. Jesus feeds the 5,000 (9:10-17)
3. Peter's confession of Jesus (9:18-21)
4. First prediction (9:22)
5. Jesus: the call to discipleship (9:23-27)

B. Jesus is the Son (9:28-50)

1. The transfiguration (9:28-36)
2. Jesus drives out an evil spirit (9:37-43a)
3. Second prediction (9:43b-45)
4. "I am the greatest" (9:46-48)
5. "We're the only ones" (9:49-50)

Part Two: The Kingdom (9:51 – 19:27)

Section Four
The Opposition to the Kingdom (9:51 – 13:21)

+ **Geographical marker:** *As the time approached for him to be taken up to heaven, Jesus resolutely set out for Jerusalem* (9:51).
+ **Important question:** *Lord, do you want us to call fire down from heaven to destroy them?* (9:54).

(For the significance of the *geographical marker* and the *important question*, see **Luke's Gospel: Part Two** on page 81.)

A. What to do when opposition comes (1) (9:51 – 10:37)

1. Samaritan opposition (9:51-56)
2. Jesus and potential disciples (9:57-62)
3. Jesus sends out seventy-two disciples (10:1-20)
4. Jesus and his Father (10:21-24)
5. The parable of the good Samaritan (10:25-37)

B. What to do when opposition comes (2) (10:38 – 11:36)

1. Jesus at Martha and Mary's (10:38-42)
2. Jesus teaches about prayer (11:1-13)
3. Jesus is accused of working with Satan (11:14-28)
4. Jesus teaches about judgment (11:29-32)
5. Jesus urges generosity (11:33-36)

C. God is Father as well as Judge (11:37 – 12:48)

1. Jesus condemns the Pharisees and the scribes (11:37-54)
2. Fear God and confess Jesus (12:1-12)
3. The parable of the rich fool (12:13-21)
4. Don't worry and trust God (12:22-34)
5. Disciples keep serving Jesus (12:35-48)

D. Make sure which side you're on (12:49 – 13:21)

1. Jesus promises division (12:49-53)
2. Jesus tells us to live wisely (12:54-59)
3. Jesus tells us to repent (13:1-9)
4. Jesus heals on the Sabbath (13:10-17)
5. Jesus promises growth (13:18-21)

Section Five
The Citizens of the Kingdom (13:22 – 17:19)

+ **Geographical marker:** *Then Jesus went through the towns and the villages, teaching as he made his way to Jerusalem (13:22).*
+ **Important question:** *Lord, are only a few people going to be saved? (13:23).*

(For the significance of the *geographical marker* and the *important question*, see **Luke's Gospel: Part Two** on page 81.)

A. Jews and Gentiles who count the cost (13:22 – 14:35)

1. The narrow door and the messianic banquet (13:22-30)
2. Jesus' sorrow over Jerusalem (13:31-35)
3. Jesus at a Pharisee's house (14:1-14)
4. The parable of the great banquet (14:15-24)
5. The cost of discipleship (14:25-35)

B. ...who know they were lost (15:1-32)

1. The Pharisees and the scribes (15:1-2)
2. The parable of the lost sheep (15:3-7)
3. The parable of the lost coin (15:8-10)
4. The parable of the lost son (15:11-24)
5. What happened to the older brother (15:25-32)

C. ...and who want to live wisely (16:1 – 17:19)

1. The parable of the wise manager (16:1-9)
2. Jesus teaches about God's wisdom (16:10-18)
3. The parable of the rich man and Lazarus (16:19-31)
4. Wisdom in the Jesus community (17:1-10)
5. Jesus heals ten lepers (17:11-19)

Section Six
The Arrival of the Kingdom (17:20 – 19:27)

+ **Geographical marker:** *Now on his way to Jerusalem, Jesus travelled along the border between Samaria and Galilee (17:11).*
+ **Important question:** *Once, on being asked by the Pharisees when the kingdom of God would come, Jesus replied... (17:20).*

(For the significance of the *geographical marker* and the *important question*, see **Luke's Gospel: Part Two** on page 81.)

A. What to do till the kingdom comes (1) (17:20 – 18:17)

1. The kingdom of God is now (17:20-21)
2. The kingdom of God is coming (17:22-37)
3. The parable of the persistent widow (18:1-8)
4. The parable of the Pharisee and the tax collector (18:9-14)
5. Jesus and the little children (18:15-17)

B. What to do till the kingdom comes (2) (18:18 – 19:27)

1. Jesus and the rich ruler (18:18-30)
2. Third prediction (18:31-34)
3. Jesus heals a blind man (18:35-43)
4. Jesus calls Zacchaeus the tax collector (19:1-10)
5. The parable of the ten minas (19:11-27)

Part Three: The Climax (19:28 – 24:53)

Section Seven
Judgment on Israel (19:28 – 21:38)

Introduction: Jesus arrives in Jerusalem (19:28-44)

A. Jesus debates with the religious leaders (19:45 – 20:40)

1. Jesus clears the temple (19:45-48)
2. The authority of Jesus questioned (20:1-8)
3. The parable of the tenants (20:9-19)
4. Paying taxes to Caesar (20:20-26)
5. Marriage at the resurrection (20:27-40)

B. Jesus announces God's judgment (20:41 – 21:38)

1. A question about the Messiah (20:41-44)
2. Warning about the scribes (20:45-47)
3. The widow's offering (21:1-4)
4. The destruction of the temple (21:5-33)
5. The end of all things (21:34-38)

Section Eight
Jesus: Saviour and King (22:1 – 24:53)

A. Jesus: teaching and alone (22:1-53)

1. Plans against Jesus (22:1-6)
2. The last supper (22:7-23)
3. Jesus teaches after the supper (22:24-38)
4. Jesus prays on the Mount of Olives (22:39-46)
5. Jesus arrested (22:47-53)

B. Jesus: condemned and crucified (22:54 – 23:56)

1. Peter denies Jesus (22:54-62)
2. The four trials (22:63 – 23:25)
3. The crucifixion (23:26-43)
4. The death of Jesus (23:44-49)
5. The burial of Jesus (23:50-56)

C. Jesus: risen and ascended (24:1-53)

1. The women meet the angels at the empty tomb (24:1-8)
2. Peter at the empty tomb (24:9-12)
3. The road to Emmaus (24:13-35)
4. Jesus appears to all the disciples (24:36-49)
5. The ascension of Jesus (24:50-53

The Matthew Experiment

How Matthew's Gospel can help you know Jesus better

Andrew Page

Are you looking for a new way of getting to know Jesus better? A great place to start is to get into one of the four Gospels. This book is designed to help us to do just that. After writing books about Mark's Gospel and about John's Gospel, Andrew Page has now turned his attention to the Gospel of Matthew.

The Matthew Experiment is two things. First, it's a basic commentary: Andrew unpacks the message of Matthew by teaching through the Gospel from beginning to end. And second, it's an invitation: the book explains how readers can learn the order of the incidents in Matthew, and so try the experiment of using what they have learnt to help them meditate their way through the Gospel. This stems from Andrew's conviction that Matthew wrote not only to give us information about Jesus, but also to help us to meet him.

Would you like to give it a try? If your answer is Yes, The Matthew Experiment is the book for you.

ISBN 978-3-95776-069-2
Pb. • 184 pp. • £ 10.00

VTR Publications
info@vtr-online.com
http://www.vtr-online.com

The Mark Experiment

How Mark's Gospel can help you know Jesus better

Andrew Page

If you are looking for a new way into Mark's Gospel and you long to allow the Gospel to help you worship and experience Jesus, *The Mark Experiment* is the book for you.

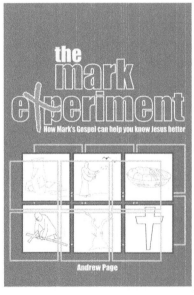

In *The Mark Experiment* Andrew Page shows you how to commit the Gospel to memory and explains how learning to meditate on the Gospel events has transformed his relationship with Jesus. Think what this might mean for your understanding of the life and ministry of Jesus.

One exciting result of this book has been the development of an innovative drama in which a team of 15 Christians from a church or student group acts out every incident in the Gospel of Mark as theatre-in-the-round. The Mark Drama is now being performed in many countries around the world.

www.themarkdrama.com

ISBN 978-3-937965-21-5
Pb. • 106 pp. • £ 8.00

VTR Publications
info@vtr-online.com
http://www.vtr-online.com

The John Experiment

How John's Gospel can help you know Jesus better

Andrew Page

Are you looking for a new way into the Gospels? Whether you have been a Christian for many years or are just considering the Christian faith, John's Gospel is a great place to start.

In The John Experiment Andrew Page unpacks John's Gospel and shows you how to commit it to memory. He explains how learning to meditate on the Gospel events is transforming his relationship with Jesus.

Would you like to give it a go? If your answer is Yes, then The John Experiment is the book for you.

ISBN 978-3-95776-070-8
Pb. • 146 pp. • £ 9.50

VTR Publications
info@vtr-online.com
http://www.vtr-online.com

The 5 Habits of
Deeply Contented People

Andrew Page

Have you found contentment?
Most people are looking for it.
If you're not, it may be because you've given up...

If you are searching or want to start your search again, *The 5 Habits of Deeply Contented People* is the book for you.

The Bible says that everyone is made in God's image. Andrew Page says there are 5 habits which express that image of God in us. He says "If we can work out what these habits mean in practice for us as individuals, we will experience a deeper level of contentment."

Basing what he writes on the second chapter of the Bible, and making clear that these habits work even if we don't believe in God, Andrew invites his readers to try out the habits for themselves.

• Do you want to be more contented, whatever life throws at you?
• Are you curious to know what it means to be made in God's image?
• Would you like to find out if the 5 habits work?

If you have said Yes to any of these questions, *The 5 Habits of Deeply Contented People* is a great place to start.

ISBN 978-3-95776-009-8
Pb. • 52 pp. • £ 7.00

VTR Publications
info@vtr-online.com
http://www.vtr-online.com

Read Mark
in 30 Days

Andrew Page

The Christian message claims that God came into our world in a man called Jesus.

But is it true?

Many people who ask that question have never read any of the source documents: they are the four Gospels in the New Testament. All of them were written in the first century.

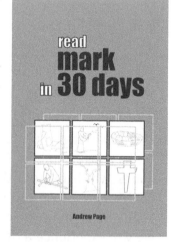

If you're an honest sceptic, or just wanting to know more about Jesus, reading Mark's Gospel is a great place to start.

In **Read Mark in 30 Days** Andrew Page suggests a passage in Mark to read for each day, adding a few comments of his own, designed to help us understand Mark's message.

After 30 days you'll have read through the whole Gospel. And be in a much better position to answer the question *Is it true?*

ISBN 978-3-95776-098-2
Pb. • 34 pp. • £ 5.00

VTR Publications
info@vtr-online.com
http://www.vtr-online.com

How to Lead Group Bible Study so that People Meet God

Andrew Page

Are you part of a Christian small group? Does your church or CU offer training to those who lead group Bible study? Do you know people who want help in how to prepare and lead group Bible study?

If you are looking for practical training in this area, *How to Lead Group Bible Study so that People Meet God* is the book for you.

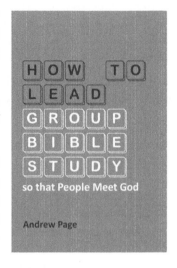

Andrew Page believes that small group Bible study can be a supernatural event. A graduate of London School of Theology, Andrew was a missionary in Austria for 20 years, working with the Austrian Christian student movement (IFES) and later pastoring a church in Innsbruck.

This is unashamedly a how-to book. Andrew has trained many people in Christian Unions and in churches, both in Austria and in the UK, and now for the first time the material is available as a book.

So, 3 questions before you buy this book:
- Do you want to start leading group Bible study?
- If you already lead group Bible study, do you want to do it better?
- Do you want to help others to learn to lead group Bible study?

If you have said Yes to any of these questions, *How to Lead Group Bible Study so that People Meet God* is a great place to start.

ISBN 978-3-95776-130-9
Pb. • 60 pp. • £ 7.50

VTR Publications
info@vtr-online.com
http://www.vtr-online.com

How to Teach the Bible so that People Meet God

Andrew Page

Andrew Page believes that Bible teaching can be a supernatural event. A graduate of London School of Theology, Andrew was a missionary in Austria for 20 years, working with the Austrian Christian student movement (IFES) and later pastoring a church in Innsbruck.

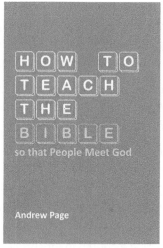

He says "Two enemies of Christian churches are Bible teaching with little biblical content and Bible teaching which is more a lecture than an event." If you agree with this, *How to Teach the Bible so that People Meet God* is the book for you.

This is unashamedly a how-to book. Andrew has trained others in this method of teaching a Bible passage in a number of countries around Europe, and now for the first time the method is available as a book.

So, 3 questions before you buy this book:
• Do you want to find out if God has given you the gift of teaching?
• Do you want to grow in the gift you believe you have?
• Do you want to help a friend to develop as a Bible teacher?

If you have said *Yes* to any of these questions, *How to Teach the Bible so that People Meet God* is a great place to start.

ISBN 978-3-95776-035-7
Pb. • 64 pp. • £ 7.50

VTR Publications
info@vtr-online.com
http://www.vtr-online.com